Also by Sylvia Browne

THE MYSTICAL LIFE OF JESUS

INSIGHT

PHENOMENON

PROPHECY

VISITS FROM THE AFTERLIFE

SYLVIA BROWNE'S BOOK OF DREAMS

PAST LIVES, FUTURE HEALING

BLESSINGS FROM THE OTHER SIDE

LIFE ON THE OTHER SIDE

THE OTHER SIDE AND BACK

ADVENTURES OF A PSYCHIC

Psychic Children

SYLVIA BROWNE

written with Lindsay Harrison

Psychic Children

REVEALING THEIR INTUITIVE GIFTS AND HIDDEN ABILITIES

PIATKUS

Copyright © 2007 by Sylvia Browne

First published in the USA in 2006 by Dutton, a member of Penguin Group (USA) Inc.

First published in Great Britain in 2007 by
Piatkus Books Ltd
5 Windmill Street
London W1T 2JA
e-mail: info@piatkus.co.uk

The moral right of the author has been asserted

*A catalogue record for this book is
available from the British Library*

ISBN 978 0 7499 2805 6

Designed by Eve L. Kirch

This book has been printed on paper manufactured with respect for the environment using wood from managed sustainable resources

Data manipulation by Phoenix Photosetting, Chatham, Kent

Printed and bound in Great Britain by
Mackays of Chatham, Chatham, Kent

From Sylvia:

To my three precious grandchildren,
Angelia, Willy, and Jeffrey

From Lindsay:

To Mom, a belated Happy 92nd Birthday

CONTENTS

ACKNOWLEDGMENTS

In addition to Brian Tart, president of Dutton, and our agent Bonnie Solow, Lindsay and I want to expess our heartfelt gratitude to every one of you—more than two thousand in total—who were generous enough to take the time to send us stories of your own psychic children. We read every one of them, and while I couldn't personally respond to them all, it's my hope that this book will bring you answers, comfort, helpful information, insight, and smiles—and again, my thanks.

God bless you.
Sylvia

INTRODUCTION

This is a book I've been preparing and looking forward to for a very long time.

My formal work as a psychic, researcher, master hypnotist, past life regressionist, lecturer, and spiritual teacher has taken me all over the world for more than half a century. But I've noticed a remarkable increase in the past ten years in the number of parents who come to me for help and advice about their children, wondering if it's possible that they might have a psychic child on their hands. The parents' reactions range from scared to confused to worried to fascinated to, in the rarest cases, delighted. Their children tell stories of imaginary friends who seem far too real; visits from spirits they later recognize as deceased family members; Angels rescuing them or just making an appearance to say hello; detailed memories of other mommies and daddies and lives in other times and other places; dreams about past, present, and future events that happen to be completely accurate; knowledge of where they lived before they came here; and a variety of abilities that far exceed the limits of our five physical senses. The parents don't understand what's happening, why it's happening, or what to do about it. This book is for them, and for all of you who find yourselves in the same confused and confusing situation.

You want to know if your child is psychic.

The answer is "Yes, they are."

All children are psychic. In the pages that follow you'll learn why that always has been and always will be true and perfectly normal. You'll learn the many ways their psychic gifts can manifest themselves, the best and worst ways to respond to those gifts, and how to most effectively teach and be taught by your psychic child. And above all, you'll learn that at the core of these wonderful gifts is exactly what lies at the core of life itself: the sacred, perfect, all-loving presence of God.

As the past ten years have unfolded, I've wondered time and again why more parents than ever are showing up at my proverbial door to share their joys and concerns about their psychic child. There's nothing new about children being born psychically gifted, so why the increase in parents who want to talk about them? Are people finally becoming more comfortable with the idea of openly discussing psychic issues that are occurring in their own homes? Are advanced spirits coming to earth in greater numbers as part of this world's ongoing spiritual awakening, with the result that our children are more psychic than ever before? Or are we within distant sight of the end of life on earth, during which the veil between this dimension and the dimension of the Other Side will slowly but surely dissipate like a fine mist, leaving us all in the perpetual God-given glory of Home?

During these ten years, through countless clients, travels all over the world, and many other books, I've been gathering my thoughts, notes, research, and stories for *Psychic Children*. May it provide answers, hope, faith, and peace to you and the psychic children with whom you share them.

—Sylvia C. Browne

The most beautiful thing we can experience is the mysterious. It is the source of all true art and all science. He to whom this emotion is a stranger, who can no longer pause to wonder and stand rapt in awe, is as good as dead: his eyes are closed.

—Albert Einstein

Psychic Children

CHAPTER ONE

Psychic Children:
God's Eternal Miracle

When my granddaughter Angelia was six years old, she had a dream. She was on the Other Side, quietly walking through the Orientation Center, a breathtaking oblong temple where spirits returning Home were talking to spirits about to leave for another lifetime on earth.

She found herself at the door to a room with a vast wall of veiled glass. Curious, she started to step inside, and got a brief glimpse of babies, for as far as her eyes could see, all of them happy and playing, while grown-ups moved among them, taking care of them.

My Spirit Guide Francine stopped her from entering the room. "You can't go in there, Angelia," Francine told her. "The babies are getting ready to leave."

I asked Angelia what she thought her dream meant.

She let out an impatient little sigh. Sometimes her Bagdah, as she's called me from the moment she could talk, is so dense. "We can't come be babies on earth until we get *little*, Bagdah."

Francine informed me later that it wasn't a dream at all, that Angelia had actually made one of her frequent astral trips to the Other

1

Side while she slept, and Francine, as always, had kept a close eye on her while she was there.

"You mean that's true?" I asked Francine. "Our spirits literally get smaller before we enter the womb? Why haven't you told me that before?"

She responded with an answer I've heard a million times. "If you don't ask the question, I can't give you the answer."

Now, in case you think these are just the ravings of a madwoman and her imaginative granddaughter, let me share an excerpt from an e-mail I received from Caroline in response to my request for stories about psychic children:

"When my oldest child was three and able to form sentences, he pointed to a portrait in our living room of his maternal grandmother, who died before he was born, and began telling me all about how much fun she was and how 'big' her laugh was. I was shocked, since he'd obviously never met her (she did have a very 'big' laugh, by the way!) and I couldn't remember anyone ever explaining to him who the lady in the portrait was, so I asked him how he knew her.

"He said, 'Because she took care of me and the other babies before we were born.' He went on to describe how she would play with the children, about ten of them, and give them lots of love and hugs. And he repeated, 'You know. When we weren't born yet.' "

So there you have it, the real answer to the question, "Where do babies come from?" They come from a vast room with a veiled glass wall on the Other Side, where they go to play and be loved and cared for while they diminish in size to be born into their new incarnations.

You also have the real answer to the question, "Why are all children psychic?"

Since my own psychic childhood in Kansas City, Missouri, my

greatest passion has been researching, studying, and psychically exploring the fact—and it is a fact—that God promised each of us eternal lives when He created us, and He's kept that promise. Our spirits, like the infinite universe we inhabit, always have been and always will be. Birth and death are not a beginning and an end, they're simply events, designed by us and our Creator, in a perfect, unending continuum. We arrive here from our real lives on the Other Side, experience this rough boot camp called life on earth for the further growth of our souls, and then head Home again with greater wisdom and depth than we had before.

Skeptics say, "Prove it."

I say, "Open your minds and talk to a child. They're all the proof you need."

Taken out of the context of eternity, the reality of psychic children can seem like an eerie, haphazard, inexplicable quirk of nature— even the devil's work, an indictment that's been hurled at me so often that I'm tempted to ask my detractors to please come up with something more original. Out of context, babies are blank slates when they're born, except for their inherited genetic influences, and they're shaped by some combination of genetics and their environment. The debate rages on about how that combination works exactly, and why so many children seem to be reflections of neither genetics nor their environment.

But in the context of eternity, and the amazing journey that leads to the arrival of a newborn, there is no debate, and there are no unanswered questions. Like everything else in God's perfect creation, it's simple, sacred logic.

Imagine this:

You're thirty years old, leading a busy, stimulating, blissfully happy life. Your career reflects your most passionate interests, and your social life is limitless in its choices. You're surrounded by loving friends, kindred spirits, and yes, even your soulmate. You live in the home of your dreams, set amidst beauty that takes your breath away. Not a moment passes when you don't feel blessed.

As often happens when we're at our confident, grateful best, you find yourself yearning to explore new territories and expand your knowledge—content as you are, you're too energized to be complacent, and you never want to stop growing. You have some very specific areas of study you want to focus on, and you know that mastering them will benefit you and everyone else around you.

There's only one catch: Those courses are only being offered in one notoriously difficult school, in a foreign land where everything will seem unfamiliar to you. It will mean leaving this beautiful life and these beautiful companions for a while, to travel to a place where there are no guarantees of the beauty, kindness, and love you're accustomed to, where the locals speak a language you'll have to learn from scratch, where you're likely to feel frightened, homesick, and very much alone, at least until you become acclimated, if ever.

Overwhelming as the prospect is, you also know it's an opportunity you can't and won't let yourself pass up. You buy yourself a round trip ticket, guaranteeing that you'll be back, and you meticulously plan every large and small detail of your time away to be sure you'll accomplish every goal you've set for yourself. And finally, surrounded by supportive loved ones who promise to stay in touch, you leave, determined, exhilarated, as prepared as you can be, and, sure enough, already homesick to the core of your soul as you bravely embark on this essential journey. When you reach your destination, your memories of home are clear as a bell and nourishing. You go back to visit every chance you get, and it thrills you when anyone from home comes to visit you.

Sooner or later, though, your new surroundings become familiar, you get to know the new people around you and learn their language, and the challenge of this difficult school consumes you. Your memories of home fade as you begin accomplishing the goals you meticulously mapped out for yourself. But in quiet moments you're aware of a deep perpetual sadness, no matter how well things are going, and you resonate with the simple truth that you still are and always will be homesick.

That's a simplified but accurate description of the journey of a newborn baby. It was your journey and mine before we came here, and it will be your journey if you choose to make the trip to this challenging school called life on earth again. As for me, I'm on my fifty-second incarnation, and when I go Home this time I intend to stay put.

My book *Life on the Other Side* offers a detailed look at our real lives, in the glorious perfection of Home. And to understand the pure logic of all children's psychic abilities, you need to understand that blissful, sacred world they've temporarily left behind toward the growth and education of their souls.

The Other Side is right here among us, an absolute mirror image of earth's topography in its original perfection, just three feet above our own ground level. Its vibrational frequency is so much higher than ours that we don't perceive its presence, and it truly is another dimension where such earthly concepts as time, gravity, space, and the laws of physics simply don't exist. When we leave these flawed, silly contraptions called bodies we return to our natural spirit forms in that glorious nearby dimension and continue our busy, stimulating, productive lives in the constant, immediate presence of God.

I started my hypothetical example with a reference to being thirty years old for a simple reason: On the Other Side, no matter what age we were when we left our physical bodies, we're all thirty years old. I know. You're wondering, "Why thirty?" I did. Everyone does. The first time my Spirit Guide Francine announced this fact to me, I asked her, "Why are we all thirty years old?" To which she replied, "Because we are." I couldn't think of a good follow-up question after that response, so I've never asked again. We're thirty years old on the Other Side because we are. It's apparently no more complicated than that.

We thirty-year-old spirits of Home have the careers of our choosing, careers in which we thrive that never for a moment feel like work. We have brilliant, limitless social lives, every recreational option we enjoy here on earth that doesn't involve harm or aggression, and the homes of our dreams that we create with simple thought projection. Our passion for learning, research, and study is satisfied by the presence of every word ever written, every work of art ever produced, every piece of music ever composed, every architectural masterpiece ever built on earth. Even treasures that have been destroyed here, or vandalized, or compromised by time, wars, and the elements, are flawlessly preserved on the Other Side and at our disposal. The great libraries of Alexandria have survived the flames that consumed them in Egypt centuries ago. The Venus de Milo is completely intact. The Dead Sea Scrolls look newly printed. And I promise you, we'll arrive Home to see the Twin Towers of the World Trade Center glistening triumphantly in the vibrant pastels of natural light, more proof that the vicious hatred that destroyed them here pales in comparison to the love of God that is utterly indestructible.

We even have unlimited access to the sacrosanct Akashic Records, the entire written body of God's knowledge, laws, and memories, housed in a white marble Greco-Roman masterpiece called the Hall or Temple of Records, one of the magnificent buildings that greet us when we first return to the Other Side.

There are some lessons, though, that can't be taught through books, or in an atmosphere of constant, pervasive love. As Francine has asked me so often when I cried to her in deep emotional pain, "What have you learned when times were good?" We accomplish some of our best growth, sadly enough, by confronting and overcoming such human-made flaws as negativity, anger, hatred, greed, violence, and faithlessness. And our eternal spirits were created with our own innate potential, coupled with a destiny to reach that potential. Achieving our unique greatness is a birthright from our Creator, a goal that drives our spirits to grow and learn and excel as powerfully as God's love itself. And so, from time to time, we choose to take brief trips away from Home to fulfill our promise to God at the moment of our creation that we will insist on being nothing less than the greatest possible manifestation of the gifts He gave us.

We incarnate with specific goals in mind, and to ensure our success we write an incredibly specific, meticulously detailed chart, planning every aspect of our trip to earth. Yes, we literally write a chart, on parchment scrolls, in Aramaic, our native tongue on the Other Side. In that chart we choose our parents and siblings. We choose exactly what we'll look like. We choose the place, date, and even the time of our birth—i.e., we even map out our own astrology charts before we come. We choose our friends, lovers, spouses, children, coworkers, enemies, passing acquaintances, and past-life reacquaintances. We choose our career paths and our missteps, our various moves throughout our lives, our health fluctuations and crises, our best and worst character traits, our talents, our areas of weakness and incompetence, and our special mental and physical challenges. There's not a single bit of trivia we overlook in our chart as we ensure our success on this brief visit to earth. And the more difficult the chart, the more advanced the spirit who wrote it. Please, please never look at another physically or mentally challenged person, child or adult, and think God is punishing them, or that it's a sign of bad karma from past lives catching up with them. Remember that they had the courage and exceptional spiritual insights to choose those challenges themselves, for some great purpose in this life, and regard them with the highest respect.

We choose our Spirit Guide from among the spirits around us on the Other Side before we depart for earth, to be our constant companion, helpmate, and life coach while we're here.

We recruit the specific Angels who will watch over us with special attention, although the whole powerful legion of Angels from all eight levels of that sacred, singular species is around us all and protecting us all throughout our lifetimes.

We even choose a totem, which is a member of the vast animal kingdom on the Other Side that we ask to guard us and comfort us on our rough journey. Never doubt that animals are held in utterly reverent esteem at Home, and we wouldn't dream of leaving without one of those pure, unflinchingly loyal spirit creatures at our side.

And finally, after an audience with our messiah and a brief, divine glimpse of Azna, the materialized presence of the Mother God, we lie down on a smooth, comfortable table in a room in the Towers, where we're eased into a twilight sleep.

During which, to quote Angelia, we "get *little*, Bagdah."

To summarize, then, in the simplest possible terms: Every child born on earth is psychic because they arrive directly from the spirit world of the Other Side. They're tuned to the spirit world because they've just been part of it. It's no more peculiar than our being most familiar with, and most easily recognizing, the people and language of our home town for quite some time after we've moved on.

And, of course, just as we inevitably adapt to new surroundings after we've left the familiar comfort of home, children inevitably make the transition from the spirit world and acclimate themselves to the gravity-challenged confines of living in a human body on earth. Some will maintain a conscious connection to the spirit world throughout their lives and grow into psychic adults. Others will gradually lose that connection before they reach puberty and forget it ever existed. There is no average age at which a child either hits some kind of psychic peak, begins to lose their spirit world connection, or decides to retain it into adulthood. Every child is unique, every child's progress is unique, and every child's chart is unique. The one common bond you can count on is that every one of them is psychic because they're still more a part of the spirit world they've just left behind than they are a part of this world on earth. All the adults you know, all the adults you see around you were once psychic children. You were once a psychic child, whether or not you remember it or ever communicated it to anyone around you.

Throughout this book, by the way, you'll be reading letters from parents, relatives, and friends of psychic children, and you may notice that a lot of the psychic children referred to are three years old. Please don't get the mistaken impression that the majority of children are at their most psychic when they're three. The only reason the age of three comes up as often as it does is that most three-year-old children are simply better able to cohesively verbalize their thoughts than they could when they were younger. If and when a child's ability peaks, fades away, or continues into adulthood isn't determined by averages or median ages. It's determined by the utterly unique chart they wrote before they came here.

So now, in addition to knowing what's been going on in the eternal life of the supposed blank slate called a newborn in the hours and eons before you caught your first glimpse of it, you also know why I have a hard time keeping a straight face in any heated genetics vs. environment debate. Every child, including you when you were an infant, chose each minute detail of each circumstance of their lifetime to propel a meticulously orchestrated agenda while they're here. There's nothing haphazard about it, or about anything in God's creation, no mysterious fluctuating percentage of genetics and environment that's invariably a euphemism for "We don't have a clue," no whimsy or luck of the draw. One illegitimate child grows up to be Leonardo da Vinci, one of the most brilliant artists, inventors, teachers, and scholars the world has ever known. Another illegitimate child grows up to be Ted Bundy, one of history's most prolific serial killers. One abusive father raises the genius composer Ludwig van Beethoven. Another abusive father raises John Wayne Gacy, who killed thirty-three young men and boys before he was executed. Why? Because da Vinci, Bundy, Beethoven, Gacy, and all the rest of us carefully dictated the genetics, environment, and countless other factors that would satisfy our unique destinies. Not the other way around.

If you're familiar with my work at all, you're aware that I don't pull any punches with any of you. And I'm sure that's why many of you refuse to pull any punches with me either. Which is one of countless reasons that an e-mail from a woman named Janie meant the world to me and why I'm so eager to share excerpts of it with you at this particular moment in this chapter. I'll dedicate it to all of you who just read the above account of our lives at Home and dismissed it as the most inane, improbable bunch of blather you've ever heard:

"I've read Sylvia's books for years, but I've always had a difficult time with her descriptions of the Other Side, and I finally put her books away. I hadn't given it any thought again until my father died a year ago. In my grief I still didn't reach for those books, but I was desperately searching for some kind of comforting sign.

"Shortly after my father's death I took my twelve-year-old son, Stuart, shopping, trying to distract him because he was suffering the same loss I was. As we rode along in the car I asked him as casually as I could where he believed Granddad was. Stuart had attended Catholic school since he was five years old, and I expected to hear a few words about heaven or hell, nothing more.

"Instead, he instantly became so excited and nervous that he couldn't sit still. He said that he knew where Granddad was, but he wasn't supposed to know any of this, wasn't supposed to tell and didn't even know how he knew, that it was coming from somewhere else and not from him. He then started telling me all about it, talking a mile a minute, and I wrote it all down the minute we got home, if only to let him know that I was taking him seriously and cared very much what he had to say. I put it away in a journal I was keeping of signs from my dad since his passing and left it there.

"Many months later I turned on the TV and there was Sylvia on *The Montel Williams Show*. I didn't pay much attention until I heard her say something about a grassy meadow when we first arrive on the Other Side. It rang a faint bell, although I wasn't sure why, and I eventually ended up digging out my journal and reading Stuart's words again.

"The more I read the more I knew I had to get out Sylvia's book *Life on the Other Side* that I'd found so unbelievable. I was amazed when I compared Sylvia's description with Stuart's.

"Here is what I wrote down that day, in my son's own words:

∗ When you go you see a grassy meadow.

∗ It is another world like our world and it's right beside us.

∗ We wait there until God says it's okay, then we come back in another body and do it over and over again.

∗ We have physical bodies here and spiritual bodies there. The atoms and molecules are different.

∗ They can see us but we can't see them.

∗ They can come to us in dreams. Granddad comes to you in dreams.

∗ We can see them sometimes in the shadows like when Dad sees a shadow in the corner of his eye.

∗ Granddad is a carpenter there like he was here. He builds bird houses.

∗ From what you are there you bring your skills here. When you go back you can be the best there at what you do.

∗ You bring skills you have there to share with people here, like singers do.

∗ There is no religion there; there is a temple where everyone goes.

∗ We stay the same age.

∗ When people here see the person they knew they're the same age you remember them.

∗ We come here to learn. We take back what we learn to God.

∗ There's no children. We don't 'do it' over there [a smirk].

∗ We can have whatever kind of house we want.

✳ We are not supposed to remember all of this.

✳ There is no hell. God accepts everyone. (He didn't learn that in Catholic school!)

✳ Granddad is right here with you wherever you go. He follows you around.

"If all that wasn't enough to make me think I had misjudged Sylvia's book, I remembered what I thought was maybe the most ridiculous statement in *Life on the Other Side* and decided to ask Stuart about it.

"I asked him where this place, heaven, or the Other Side, was. I pointed at the ceiling and asked if it was up there. He said no, it was here, and he held his hand up just past his knees. I tried not to act surprised and said, 'Oh, it's off the ground?' And he said, 'Yes. About three feet.'

"It's nearly a year since my son shared all that information, and I'm sad to say that he remembers very little of it. He did say a few months ago that Granddad was reborn as a little boy in China, but I told him to stop being ridiculous. Maybe this time he was making it up."

Remember, Janie, you put *Life on the Other Side* away because you thought it was ridiculous and that I was making it up. Then your son confirmed it all, with no help from me. Since that somehow failed to keep the word *ridiculous* out of your vocabulary, let me return the favor for Stuart: Your father was reborn as a boy in China a few months ago. You owe your son an apology.

Like all of us who travel to a strange place from a home we love, children are naturally more connected to Home than to earth when they arrive. They've just made a trip from one dimension to another, after all, so it makes all the sense in the world that they're still tuned to the higher frequency of the Other Side. Of course they can see and hear residents of the spirit world. They were residents of it themselves not long ago. In fact, like all of us, they're far more accustomed to living There than here. I don't care how many times we've reincarnated, or how long each of those incarnations lasted, our total number of years on earth are the blink of an eye compared to our eternity at Home. In computer terms (or so I'm told—computers and I have made a mutual agreement to stay away from each other), the world of the Other Side is our default. Our lives on earth are anomalies.

Right about now a question may be occurring to you that's fair, reasonable, and logical: If we came from this idyllic place, and these idyllic lives, and we have them to look forward to when we die, why doesn't God see to it that we remember them throughout our lifetimes here? It would make faith in Him so much easier, and make the thought of death so much less frightening.

I've asked my Spirit Guide Francine that same question more than once. And the best answer seems to be that if we really did have easy access to our memories of the Other Side, our earthly lives would seem virtually unbearable by comparison. We would never bother to adapt and accomplish the goals we've set for ourselves, and chances are we'd all go racing back there in a heartbeat instead of putting ourselves through the fear, greed, violence, hatred, inequity, war, dishonesty, and pervasive uncertainty that simply don't exist in that Place we came from.

I don't have a dark enough impression of life on earth to mean this analogy literally, but if you've ever talked to a prisoner of war as I have, you've been told that in order to retain their sanity, they learn not to obsess about the lives from which they've been separated, because it would make their lives in captivity completely unbearable. They focus as best they can on surviving from one day to the next, maintaining as much faith and hope of freedom as they're able to but indulging as little as possible in fantasies of what they'd be doing right that moment if they were home. The choices come down to making the most of a terrible situation or losing their minds. No other options are available.

Now, obviously, we all had the option not to come here at all. And even those of us who are living lives that are unimaginably awful are living those lives by their own design, for reasons that will make all the sense in the world when we're Home again. God bless us all for having the courage, and for holding fast to the faith in Him that keeps our path to the Other Side unobstructed, even without ready access to the crystal clear memories that would prove the exquisite eternity that is our birthright.

Indigo, Crystal, and Rainbow Children

I can't even count the number of e-mails I received from people announcing that they either have or grew up themselves as an Indigo Child or a Crystal Child or a Rainbow Child. I've been hearing those terms for several years now and had them explained to me many times, and from what I understand, it's thought that Indigo Children were born in 1978 or later, while Crystal Children were born in 1995 or later. Rainbow Children don't seem to have a specific year of inception, maybe because there are thought to be very few of them walking among us. Their designations as indigo or crystal or rainbow relate to the color of their auras and energy patterns, and they're considered to be the embodiments of an evolutionary leap forward for humankind.

15

The Rainbow Children, apparently, are living their first incarnation on earth, and they exclusively choose adult Crystal Children to be their parents. They're here for no other reason than to be of service.

Crystal Children are described as being wise beyond their years, with big eyes. They're limited to ages zero through seven and are "happy" and "delightful." The same authors who use those adjectives add that Crystal Children may be diagnosed with autism or Asperger's syndrome, neither of which usually includes behavioral symptoms like "happy" and "delightful," but I'm simply repeating what I've read.

Then there are Indigo Children, who are thought to be between the ages of seven and twenty-five. They have "important life purposes." (The rest of us don't?) But unlike Crystal Children, they're aggressive, they're prone to depression and addictions, and they're "independent and proud, even if they're constantly asking you for money." (Again, don't ask me, I'm just reporting.)

Entire books have been written on these three classifications of special children, so please don't think I'm claiming to represent all there is to say about the Rainbow, Crystal, and Indigo Children.

As for what I have to say about them, it can be boiled down to two words: "Stop already!"

With no disrespect intended toward the many authors, devotees, and children themselves of this concept, I don't believe a word of it, and I'm not comfortable with it. I don't understand the value of any earthly contrivance that categorizes, stereotypes, creates more separateness than unity, and implies that any child is more special than any other. There seems to be a kind of elitism about it, in a world where it's already tough enough for children—and adults too, let's face it—to feel as if they fit in, that they're welcome and appreciated, individually, for exactly who they are, without even the most well-intentioned stereotyping. Take it from a woman whose childhood was spent not fitting in, knowing I wasn't normal and feeling inappropriate because of it a great deal of the time—it can be lonely, and it can hurt.

I promise you, these manufactured labels serve no purpose except to overcomplicate things. Just call them Psychic Children, for all the reasons that every other child on earth is psychic, and leave it at that.

Old Souls and New Souls

You've heard the terms *old soul* and *new soul* countless times and possibly even used them yourself when referring to children. "Look at those eyes. Such wisdom, such an old soul," you'll hear. Or, "What an innocent, naive, happy baby. Must be a new soul." Relatively harmless assessments, just completely inaccurate.

The truth is, all souls are exactly the same age. It's not an easy concept to grasp in this earthly dimension where we're so deeply ingrained with measuring and tracking everything by a yardstick called time. We know exactly how many years old we are, how many hours of sleep we get from one night to the next, how many minutes we live from our work and our shopping centers and our favorite local restaurants, how many days per week we work—name the activity, we attach a time increment to it. Don't take this as my invitation to throw the whole idea of time out the window and use me as an excuse for being chronically late, missing deadlines, and ignoring scheduled commitments. As long as we're here we have to play by the house rules. It just makes it difficult to fathom that nowhere else in God's creation, including the Other Side, is there anything else but a perpetual now, the always-was-and-always-will-be of eternity, which makes every spirit on earth the same ageless, timeless age.

The difference we sometimes perceive between those seemingly old souls and new souls is actually a difference in the number of times they've incarnated—i.e., the number of times they've experienced life on earth and moved to another level of advancement. And make no mistake about it, we absolutely get to choose whether or not and how often we're willing to put ourselves through this boot camp. My Spirit Guide Francine incarnated once, was killed by a spear in Colombia in 1520 while trying to protect her infant child during a Spanish invasion, and decided that was quite enough incarnating for her. (Every Spirit Guide has to have incarnated at least once or they'd never be able to relate to what we on earth put ourselves through.) She's a kind, loving, brilliantly wise woman, but I can only imagine her arriving on earth as an infant and her parents trying to make sense, just for starters, of the guilelessly literal way her mind works. Ask Francine the question, "Can you describe yourself?" for example, and she will answer, "Yes." Accurate and inarguable, but not what the person asking the question had in mind.

Those of us who've been here repeatedly, and have done battle over and over again with the countless forms that earthly, human-made negativity takes, are bound to have a certain air of resigned acceptance about them, not from their age but from the relative inevitable street-smart wisdom of a spirit who's so determined to advance along their path that they just keep coming again and again and again.

And just as there are different levels of school—having nothing to do with age or the value of each student—there are different levels of advancement our spirits can achieve toward our own highest potential. One in particular is worth mentioning, because on occasion you might run across a spirit in the body of a child who is more advanced than most of us will ever aspire to be.

Mission Life Entities

Each of us, including every newborn, every toddler, every child on earth, arrives here with a meticulously charted purpose to fulfill. Our spirits never forget what that purpose is. Our Spirit Guide knows. And of course God knows. There isn't any purpose that's more highly valued by God than any other purpose—our continuing toward the finest expression of this utterly unique soul that He created for each one of us is His eternal hope, and in His eyes we never fail.

One of the most advanced purposes we can volunteer for is that of the Mission Life Entity. As a Mission Life Entity writes their chart with God's help, they essentially say to Him, "Wherever on earth you need me, I'll gladly go." The manifestation of that chart is a person—and thank God there are many of them—who will sacrifice their own physical and emotional comfort to be anywhere that calls them, to compassionately ignite, affirm, and celebrate the divine genetic legacy of the Creator in every child of God they touch. They transcend differences in religious beliefs and earthly dogmatic rhetoric. They're not here to preach or convert, nor would they ever segregate, isolate, or try to control those around them, especially not in the name of God. They don't claim to have a closer or more special relationship with God than anyone else, because they know He treasures us all. They're never superior, never spiritual snobs, and they'll pursue any occupation that's needed wherever they happen to find themselves. Their true work is simply to actively elevate the spiritual health of humanity, through words, deeds, example, grace, and unflinching faith.

Uniquely advanced as they are, they invariably write especially difficult charts for themselves, and these souls are often afflicted with childhoods that we can't imagine anyone choosing for themselves. Those same childhoods might easily scar or embitter the majority of us. But the Mission Life Entity, not more psychically connected to Home than any other child but simply more immediately conscious of it, will seem almost nourished by their hardships, seeing them as the realization of exactly what they planned and exactly what they need to fulfill their extraordinary sacred destiny.

There's infinite knowledge to be gained from every child, but if you find yourself in the presence of a little Mission Life Entity who greets every challenge with joyful courage and never waivers for a moment from their almost transcendent faith in and love of God, be their most loyal, attentive student.

Many of them have distinguished themselves in very public arenas. Abraham Lincoln was a Mission Life Entity, as was Mother Teresa, as was Pope John XXIII. But most Mission Life Entities are people you'll probably never hear of or read about in national headlines as they quietly leave their profoundly spiritual mark on all of us. And when a Mission Life Entity charts themselves to go Home when they're still children, that spiritual mark can sometimes be even more profound in its purity, simplicity, and innocence.

Mattie Stepanek was a Mission Life Entity, born in 1990. Mattie was six years old when he contracted a rare form of muscular dystrophy that had already taken the lives of his two older brothers and older sister. He wrote five bestselling books of poetry in his lifetime, was named the National Goodwill Ambassador for the Muscular Dystrophy Association and was a frequent and treasured guest on

The Oprah Winfrey Show, Larry King Live, and *Good Morning America.*

He died on June 22, 2004. He was fourteen years old and had spent half of his life in a wheelchair, enduring a tracheotomy, a ventilator, weekly blood transfusions, nightly IV fluids, and countless other extraordinary medical requirements. His funeral was attended by more than 1,300 people, and his eulogy was delivered by former president Jimmy Carter, including the words, "We have known kings and queens, and we've known presidents and prime ministers, but the most extraordinary person whom I have ever known in my life is Mattie Stepanek."

Among Mattie's poems is one entitled "Awakening After a Close Call." He wrote it at the age of eleven after a near-death experience:

Don't believe the Christmas trees!
Everything is so much more beautiful
And wonderful, and glorious
Than anything we can imagine
Or compare, or create.
Especially the Light, and the Angels!
The Light is so many things . . .
A window.
A tunnel.
A sunset at the edge
Of a polished pier.
And the Angels . . .
The Angels are more than
Just males and females with wings.
They glow with the Light
Of Every-color!

One color at a time,
Or all at once, or none at all.
But there is no darkness.
There is no darkness in Heaven.
And there is no death.
Even though we must die to enter,
As we face the Light and the Angels,
We are beyond any type of death.
Don't believe the Christmas trees!
Heaven is beyond human description.
Believe in the Spirit behind the trees!
Believe in the Life related to the decorations.
Believe in the Word leading us to our Future.
And always,
And always, and always,
Believe in the Light, and the Angels!

Mattie asked to be remembered as a "Poet, Peacemaker, and Philosopher Who Played," and his philosophy was "Remember to play after every storm."

It's worth noting that he never once referred to himself as a Mission Life Entity. I will always believe it's because he was so busy being one that he never felt the need to classify himself as one—in case you're wondering why I'm so committed to my belief in this divine label while being so skeptical of the ones we discussed earlier.

The Psychic Gifts

Psychic children, just like psychic adults, have varying specialties, some gifts that are more pronounced than others. Understanding what those specific gifts are, and how they manifest themselves, can be enormously helpful in keeping them from seeming quite so mysterious, random, and sometimes even scary if you're not expecting them. I'll be covering some of them in upcoming chapters, but for now, here are a few of the basics.

I think my granddaughter Angelia was about four years old when she casually asked one day, "Bagdah, who is the tall lady with dark hair who was in the bathroom with you?" Since I'd been in the bathroom alone, I knew she had to have seen Francine, my Spirit Guide, who's 5'9", tall and slender, with black hair she usually wears in a long thick braid that trails down her back to her waist. Angelia's ability to see Francine (and a lot of other spirits and ghosts you'll read about in later chapters) is an example of **clairvoyance**.

Clairvoyance (from the French for "clear seeing," by the way) is simply the ability to see beings, objects, or information from another dimension. Clairvoyance is not uncommon in the psychic repertoire of children—and of animals too, for that matter, which you know if you have pets who stare, bark, and/or react with happy enthusiasm to seemingly empty corners of the room.

You'll be reading many, many stories of clairvoyant children throughout this book, but for now let me just give you a couple of pieces of advice about them that my Grandmother Ada gave me when I was a clairvoyant child, and frightened by much of what I saw that was so obviously not visible to anyone else but me:

All psychic gifts, including clairvoyance, are given to us by God, just like every other gift with which we're born. They're to be honored, cherished, and used exclusively for His good or not at all.

And since God is the Source of this gift, He's the One to turn to for guidance when and if it becomes overwhelming.

I was five years old when I had my first clairvoyant experience. I was at the dinner table with my family and suddenly saw the faces of both my great-grandmothers melting like hot wax. Needless to say, it was a horrible sight, made even more horrible by the fact that everyone else at the table was going right on eating as if it was just another routine evening at the Shoemaker house.

Within two weeks, both my great-grandmothers were dead. Rather than catching on immediately that I'd clairvoyantly witnessed signs of their impending death, I thought I'd somehow made their faces melt and, as a result, killed them. I also tried to imagine a lifetime of hideous visions cropping up everywhere I turned, and I would truly have preferred death to that kind of life.

Of course Grandma Ada patiently explained clairvoyance and the real meaning of what I'd seen, which cleared my conscience. As for my fear of a nonstop parade of involuntary visions, she explained that God would help if I'd just take Him up on His promise, "Ask and it shall be given."

I prayed, promising to dedicate my gifts to Him on this earth, if in return He would only send me clairvoyant images I could put to use. If I have to clairvoyantly see a disease-ravaged body, show me whose it is and how I can either help them get better or help them make peace with their passage Home. If I have to psychically witness a plane crash, or a car accident, or a devastating fire, or the aftermath of a natural disaster, give me enough information to warn people ahead of time and, if possible, save some lives—or don't let me see those images at all.

The prayers worked, and they'll work for any child in your life who's more frightened than delighted by their clairvoyance. The same rule works here that works in every situation in life: Turn to God and let His help come shining through.

Then there's **clairaudience**, another very common psychic specialty, which is the ability to *hear* beings and information from another dimension. Again, you'll be reading wonderful stories involving clairaudience throughout this book, but if your child is having supposedly one-sided conversations with an imaginary friend (more about that later, too, you can count on it), it's a safe bet that those conversations aren't one-sided at all; your child is simply clairaudient and hearing the other side of it as clearly as you're hearing them.

Or they might just hear and repeat a cue from the Other Side that leaves you standing there gaping at them. My grandson Willy, who's the least overtly psychic member of the family, was three years old when he chimed in on a conversation about my beloved father, who died before Willy was born. First he helpfully contributed the words "Old Poppy," my sons' nickname for Daddy that I promise Willy had never heard before. Then, to the stunned amazement of all of us in the room, he beamed up at me and said, "That's my girl." If there's one phrase I associate with my dad that never ceased to make my heart soar, it was his proud, frequent, "That's my girl." That he chose my joyful, irresistible three-year-old grandson to deliver those words was the greatest confirmation I could have asked for that Daddy was there with us—I could have come up with a logical explanation for anyone else *maybe* remembering. But Willy? Other than my dad conveying it to that pure, innocent, psychic little spirit, how else could he possibly have come up with it? (Thanks again for that, Daddy. And I'm still your girl.)

Just as with clairvoyance, encouraging children to pray for God's divine guidance can turn this potentially scary psychic talent into a happy, comforting, and informative source of messages from Home.

Clairsentience can be harder to detect in both children and adults, but it can be powerful and worth watching out for. A clairsentient person has the ability to receive and actually experience the physical and emotional projections of those from both other dimensions and this one. A clairsentient in the same room with a person whose leg is broken, or who's ill, for example, might feel a very real corresponding pain in their own leg, or symptoms of the same illness. A clairsentient involved in the search for a missing person who's being hidden in a tiny, dark, cold cellar will not only perceive the cold and the darkness but will experience the same claustrophobia the missing person is going through. In the presence of a confused, depressed ghost, a clairsentient child or adult can easily take on the sensations of confusion or depression that can be mistaken for their own.

Martha e-mailed the following story about her clairsentient daughter without knowing or understanding the phenomenon:

"My four-year-old daughter, Casey, and I met an old high school acquaintance for lunch a few weeks ago. I hadn't seen him or heard from him in about twenty years, and it seemed like it would be fun to catch up and get reacquainted after all this time. Casey had been feeling great all morning, but the longer we sat there at lunch the more she started complaining that her head and tummy hurt and she barely touched her food even though she'd been telling me on the way to lunch how hungry she was. She got so sick that although I was really enjoying myself we ended up leaving the restaurant early and going home. Within a couple of hours after we got home she was fine again. As for my high school acquaintance, all she had to say was that he made her not feel good, but he'd been nothing but pleasant to both of us, so I couldn't imagine what she was talking about.

"A few months later I saw another high school friend I've stayed in touch with and told her I'd seen 'Billy.' She was shocked that I'd seen him so recently and thought he seemed fine, because not long after my lunch with him he passed away from liver disease due to chronic alcoholism.

"Is it possible that my daughter 'picked up' that he was an alcoholic and it made her so nervous she got sick? Or was she really sick and the timing was just a coincidence? I've been so confused about this. I just don't know what to think."

That's an example of a clairsentient child who wasn't directly perceiving the man's alcoholism but was literally, physically feeling the symptoms of the illness that was killing him, and she had no idea what was happening to her or why.

In the last chapter of this book I'll be giving you several Tools of Protection that you can use on and/or teach to a clairsentient child to help them separate their own physical and emotional issues from those around them—essential for the well-being of a child who's both blessed and afflicted with this gift of being almost literally empathetic to a fault.

In the meantime, what an excellent illustration of yet another reason, in addition to the all-important factor of their safety, why you should watch children very closely when they're around people they don't know, or don't know well. You're likely to learn a lot about the potential clairsentience of the children, but you're also likely to be given some good food for thought about the people in your life.

These are the most common psychic gifts you might find yourself marveling over and/or being mystified by as the children around you demonstrate that they're still in transition from Home to earth. Again, though, there is no child who is more psychic or more connected to the Other Side than any other. The only variation is in how and if they choose to express it. As the remaining chapters of this book unfold I'll share psychic story after psychic story from my family and yours, and I'll explain more specific psychic skills you'll want to watch for that those stories illustrate. My prayer for this book is that all these upcoming stories and all this upcoming information will enrich your faith in the survival of the soul and in God Himself, who breathed the miracle of eternity into each of us when He so lovingly gave us life and has walked every step of the way with us ever since.

God's eternal miracle is on open, innocent, guileless display in the psychic spirits of our children if we'll just open our minds and pay close, well-informed attention.

CHAPTER TWO

My Family:
A Legacy of Psychics

I f you know my work, or you've seen me on television, or you've
been to one of my lectures, you've heard me say a thousand times
that I come from a lineage of psychics that traceably dates back
three hundred years. And you're also aware that I'm neither the first
nor the last of the psychics in my family to devote a lifetime to these
gifts.

But what I'm hoping as you read this chapter is not that you'll
find yourself amazed at how extraordinary my family is but that
you'll recognize many of our psychic gifts in the children around you
and, as a result, learn to embrace them, encourage them, and celebrate them.

A frequent theme in the thousands of e-mails and letters I've received on the subject of psychic children is a fear that there's something evil or Godless about these gifts. Let me assure you, from the
core of my soul, that nothing could be further from the truth. God is
our foundation, our essence, our inspiration, our motivation, the
Source from which our gifts and yours were given. I once heard the
observation that "Life is God's gift to us. How we live it is our gift to

Him." Not a day goes by in my family—and I mean that literally—when we don't try to give back to Him some small measure of all He's given us through the wealth of gifts He's bestowed, psychic and otherwise. I was a psychic child, like all children. Seventy years later I don't think there's an unkind adjective that hasn't been hurled at me by those who insist on believing that psychic abilities don't exist (despite the fact that every close-minded skeptic in the world was once psychic themselves; they've just forgotten) and/or that I'm doing the devil's work. And to them I say, "Question my psychic gifts all you want, but don't *ever* question my spirituality and my commitment to God." Psychic gifts and God-centered lives coexist in my family. They always have, and they always will, until a day that will never come, when one of us starts misusing our gifts, or taking credit for them ourselves. That's the closest to evil these God-given abilities can ever get.

And I will always consider myself blessed that I was a psychic child long before it became an accepted practice to treat children who hear voices and see visions with antipsychotic drugs. Not a week goes by when I don't hear horror stories about children as young as three and four years old being given powerful mind- and mood-altering medication for no other reason than that they innocently told the truth about their interaction with the spirit world. Please, *please* read the first chapter of this book as often as it takes to understand not just how but why there's nothing more natural to a child than still being sensitive to the dimension from which they've just arrived. It's an expression of their gifts, their eternity and their genetic link to their Creator. Punishing them for it with drugs, disapproval, and embarrassment is no different than punishing them for showing an early talent at music or writing or sports or any other ability they've arrived with. When I think of this rich, blessed life I've lived in God's service by putting my psychic gifts to His best possible purpose, and the possibility that it could all have been taken away by well-intentioned but uninformed grown-ups with prescription pads in hand, it takes my breath away. For the millionth time, thank you, God and Grandma Ada, for nurturing my gifts and helping them thrive in me, even in those times when I myself would have been foolish enough to wish them away until I got it through my head that I could use them to help people.

My Psychic Childhood

I was born in Kansas City, the heart of the Bible Belt, in 1936. Neither of my parents had retained a shred of the psychic abilities they were born with, which left that confusing and often frightening part of me in the capable, empathetic hands of Ada Coil, my maternal grandmother, who'd been psychic all her life, as had many of her ancestors.

Grandma Ada was born in 1865. She was clairvoyant (she saw spirits and visions), clairaudient (she could hear and communicate with the Other Side), clairsentient (able to receive thoughts and emotions and experience them as her own), and a renowned healer. She had several Spirit Guides, whom she referred to as her "voices," but the most prominent one was named Athena. She was eons ahead of her time, doing readings in her threadbare little apartment. I spent much of my early childhood sitting quietly nearby watching a steady stream of clients from every imaginable race, creed, religion, and circumstance find solace through Grandma Ada's gifts and her extraordinary compassion. Through her eyes every person who stepped across her threshold—rich or poor, healthy or infirm, infant or ancient, devout or agnostic—was worthy of her most profound respect as children of God. She reunited them with departed loved ones. She found everything from their missing friends and family members to their missing wallets. She predicted their futures. And she was a wonderful healer. In return, she was paid based on whatever her clients could afford. Occasionally it was money. More often it was clothing, a casserole, handpicked flowers, or nothing at all. She valued each of them equally, just as she valued those who offered them.

The one healing she could never accomplish was on behalf of her son Marcus Behn, my uncle, whom we called Brother. He was stricken with cerebral palsy as a child and, according to his doctors, wasn't supposed to live past puberty. He lived with Grandma Ada all his life, and she adored him. He had a brilliant mind and an equally brilliant gentle spirit. Grandma Ada always said she'd never leave him. She died when I was eighteen, and Brother died two days later at the age of fifty-two, of what the coroner called "unknown causes." I felt my world had ended when I lost them.

I was born with a variety of psychic gifts, as all children are, and it was Grandma Ada who patiently explained them to me, always told me the truth about them, never let me forget that they were blessings from God to be used only for His finest purpose, and taught me to be grateful for them. That last one was tough for me— I can't begin to count the number of times throughout my childhood when I would have wished these gifts away, because they sometimes frightened me, sometimes got me in trouble, and sometimes made me feel isolated when I saw and heard things that no one else could see or hear. But Grandma Ada, with her singular blend of gentility and firmness, guided me safely through the rough, scary times and refused to let me turn my back on what God had given me. In fact, I was still a child when she informed me that someday I would have two sons, move to California, and become well known by carrying on her work. I laughed in her face and told her no, that I'd already decided my future, thank you: I was going to be a nun. The moral of that story, as I sit here in California with two sons, averaging twenty readings a day when I'm not traveling to appearances around the world, is that I've never met a psychic, including me, who's psychic about themselves.

In the first chapter I told the story of my first psychic vision, when the fact that both my great-grandmothers were about to die manifested itself through my eyes in their faces appearing to melt. When Grandma Ada psychically perceived an impending death, she saw the person surrounded by a blue haze. I took great comfort in her sharing her stories of the psychic experiences that had been a part of her life since she was a child. If being psychic made me more like this woman I idolized, then I was tentatively willing to tolerate it. And Grandma Ada was especially adept at making these gifts seem both sacred and practical at the same time. She never believed that God gave us these abilities for the purpose of showing off, and if we didn't put them to good use in our day-to-day lives, they were of no use at all. One of her favorite examples came from her own childhood, when her parents gave her the nightly assignment of riding on horseback to secure the stockades that surrounded and protected the property. At first glance it sounds like a dangerous chore for a little girl to undertake. But for a little girl as psychic as Ada, it made perfect sense: She was the only member of her family who always knew when the Indians from a nearby reservation might attack, and therefore the only member of her family who could reliably secure the property without putting herself at risk.

The concept of making practical use of what seemed like completely impractical gifts had an impact on me, and while I have no memory of actually seeking out opportunities to put that idea into practice, I have clear memories of the first few times it happened with no conscious effort on my part.

I was three or four years old and had made the transition from only seeing and hearing spirits in the private darkness of my bedroom to seeing and hearing them just as clearly in broad daylight. Grandma Ada had lost her steel lockbox in which she kept her important papers. She'd torn the house apart, as had the rest of us trying to help her find it, when I happened to look over at a gigantic wooden bureau in her bedroom and saw a tiny woman standing beside it, pointing to the back of it. My detailed description of the woman revealed her to be Grandma Ada's grandmother, and my description of where she was pointing prompted Grandma Ada to remember that she'd slipped her lockbox behind the bureau for safekeeping as it was moved into place years earlier.

A second incident happened when I was four years old. I'd already learned that in those rooms full of people I routinely witnessed, only some of them were part of this earthly dimension, while the rest were from the higher dimension of the Other Side, which Grandma Ada had begun explaining by then, and all of them were equally real to me. I no longer bothered to ask anyone, "Did you see that?" or "Did you hear that?" From everyone but Grandma Ada, the answer was invariably, "No," often with an added, "Knock it off, Sylvia, you're just imagining things again."

One night the family was gathered in the living room after dinner. I was sitting on the floor at Grandma Ada's feet when I saw a man materializing over her left shoulder. I whispered, "Grandma, there's a man behind you. Who is he?"

She asked what he looked like, and I told her, "He's tall, he has reddish colored hair, and he has on little round wire glasses. There's a horn thing tied to a string around his neck that he says he used to listen to people's chests."

Grandma Ada recognized him instantly and was thrilled by this visit from her Uncle Jim, a doctor who'd died twenty-four years earlier. I remember how grateful she was, and how proud I was to have provided her with a reunion with someone she'd loved so much. Between the lockbox and Uncle Jim, I was getting my first glimmers that maybe being psychic wasn't such a bad thing, if for no other reason than that I could use it to make my beloved grandmother smile that transcendent smile of hers.

And then there was the incident that led to my first appearance in the press. I was five years old, and, like all five-year-olds, beside myself with excitement about Halloween. My friend Pam and I were going trick-or-treating together, and she was coming to my house so we could show each other our costumes. As I was slipping into mine I was overcome with the most hideous vision of Pam, in her costume, bursting into flames, and my throwing her to the ground and rolling her up into a rug to put out the fire. I was frantic that maybe something had happened to her on the way to my house, so it was a huge relief when she rang the doorbell a few minutes later, happy and healthy as ever and cute as a button in her little crepe paper witch costume.

There we were, dancing and modeling and parading around the living room, neither of us paying the slightest bit of attention when Pam spent too much time whirling directly above the furnace vent in the floor, draped in highly combustible crepe paper. One minute we were giggling and playing, and an instant later my best friend was on fire, identical to the vision I'd had less than an hour before. And identical to that vision and undoubtedly instructed by it, I dived for her, pushed her to the floor and rolled her up in the closest area rug, smothering the flames. Her injuries were minor, thank God, and our local paper, the *Kansas City Star*, printed a sweet article about little five-year-old Sylvia Shoemaker saving the life of her friend. I thought the same thing about it then that I think about it now: I didn't deserve a bit of the credit. Without that vision, I wouldn't have had the first clue about what to do.

If it's any comfort to those of you whose children are very active psychically, I was not a docile, easygoing child. In fact, I'm sure I was an absolute handful who would have been medicated into a dull stupor if medicating children had been common back then and if my mother had been given a vote. I was constantly on the move and much too inquisitive and outspoken for anyone's comfort except my own. I hadn't learned to edit myself, so whatever I knew I said out loud, and I had no concept of anything being none of my business. Hence my casual announcement at the dinner table, for example, that Daddy, whom I adored, had a blonde girlfriend, and he called her at night when we were all asleep and when he went to the store. I knew exactly what she looked like, exactly how long they'd been seeing each other, and exactly where and how often they met. (Unfortunately, he and my very troubled mother never did break up. She was too mean to let him go, and he used to joke that he never left her because it would have meant kissing her good-bye.)

I routinely announced who was calling before the phone rang and who was at the door before anyone knocked. I told my mother that my daddy's father had died moments before Daddy came home to break the news to us. I pulled Daddy out of a theater one after-noon in the middle of a movie in a panic because I knew my baby sister, Sharon, was suddenly unable to breathe, and we got home with only moments to spare, the doctor said later, for Daddy to rush her to the hospital, where she was treated for nearly fatal double pneumonia. I told my friend Mary Margaret that her mother's arm would be broken and her father was going to lose his job, both of which happened within the next two months. Word was beginning to spread that "Sylvia knows things."

Having nothing to do with religion and everything to do with dis-cipline, Grandma Ada became convinced that maybe the nuns at the Catholic school in our neighborhood could introduce some or-der into my hyperactive disorderly life. It was an unorthodox sugges-tion on her part, if you'll pardon the expression, because our family at the time was a haphazard blend of Lutheran, Episcopalian, and Jewish. But no one objected, and from the moment I arrived I loved everything about it. Testing indicated that I was advanced for my age, so at the age of five I started school in the second grade. I was in awe of the nuns and the depth of their commitment to God. I was in awe of the gorgeous rituals of the church. And for the first time in my young life I didn't feel like an outsider. Grandma Ada had already taught me a lot about Angels and spirits, and here I was in a school where Angels and spirits were openly spoken about and adored. I heard about little children in mystical places like Lourdes and Fa-tima who saw visions and heard voices and took comfort in the thought that maybe I wasn't so inappropriate after all.

I no longer minded so much that I was constantly surrounded by the spirit world, day and night, although I did appreciate the flash-light Grandma Ada gave me to take to bed—spirits were easier to deal with when I could see them clearly rather than being converged upon by a busy, milling crowd of shadows. I was even getting slightly accustomed to the spirit world's very definitive voices. Spirits, as you know, live in a dimension with a higher frequency than ours here on earth. Their ability to materialize in our dimension is a bit of a challenge for them, but slowing their speech to our frequency is impossible. The result is that they sound exactly like an audiotape played on fast-forward. Until you get accustomed to it, it can be jarring, annoying, hard to understand, and, take it from me, downright terrifying when you're least expecting it, especially when you're a child.

I was seven years old, alone in my bedroom, playing with my flashlight one night as usual, when, with no warning, the glow from the flashlight began to grow and intensify until it filled the room with almost blinding white light. I was gaping at it, too mesmerized and frightened to move, when from what seemed to be the center of the light a woman's high-pitched chirping voice said, with a clarity I'd never experienced before from the spirit world, "Don't be afraid, Sylvia. I come from God."

I was out of that room and down the stairs in less than a heartbeat, screaming in terror for Grandma Ada, whom I careened into in the kitchen. Through wracking sobs I described what had happened. She quietly stroked my hair and said, "That was your Spirit Guide, sweetheart. She's here to help you."

Thus began my lifelong relationship with my constant companion, inspiration, and advisor, my Spirit Guide Francine, whose name I insisted on changing from her given name Iena because I liked the name Francine better. And I truly hope all of you who've experienced a child screaming into your arms from their bedroom, quivering in fear, will take note: Calm reassurance that the spirit who's frightened your child is visiting them from God, whether it's their Spirit Guide or just a departed loved one who's stopped by to say hello, is the kind of God-centered support that child will cherish all their life.

I was in regular communication with Francine from that night on. It's interesting that although I could see other spirits with the greatest of ease, I only got a brief glimpse of her once, years later, and even then I turned away. Other people routinely see her, including my grandchildren when they were younger, but it certainly helps to illustrate the point that no psychic, child or adult, sees every spirit in our midst.

It was probably inevitable that a combination of Francine and my big mouth got me in trouble at my beloved Catholic school, and created my first point of confusion about traditional religion. I was nine years old, and Sister Mary Stephanie was talking to the class about our guardian Angels. Truly thinking I was being helpful and confirming what she was saying, I raised my hand and announced that not only did I know my guardian Angel existed, but she talked to me. (At the time I hadn't learned the difference between guardian Angels and Spirit Guides.)

"Of course she does, dear, they talk to all of us," Sister Mary Stephanie replied, in that patronizing tone adults unfortunately use on children that translates to, "If I pretend to believe you, maybe you'll stop talking."

I didn't appreciate being humored when I was telling the truth, so I pressed on. "No," I said, "I mean she really talks to me, and I hear her. All the time."

With which Sister Mary Stephanie informed me that we'd continue this discussion after school. I knew that meant I was being punished, I just couldn't imagine what I'd done wrong. When she and I were alone later that afternoon, she demanded an explanation, and I told her about Francine and that high-pitched chirpy voice that talked to me about God and the beautiful, sacred spirit world on the Other Side after we die.

In response Sister Mary Stephanie, who taught with such reverence about God and spirits and Angels and the blessed children of Lourdes and Fatima, scolded me about causing trouble and making things up. I didn't understand then, and I don't understand now. There are spirits and Angels all around us, but if we communicate with them there's either something wrong with us or we're lying? Grandma Ada didn't understand it either, when I finally got home and asked her to explain why I'd been punished. In fact, she stormed out of the house and off to a long face-to-face talk with Sister Mary Stephanie. She never gave me the details of their conversation, but I was never scolded for hearing voices again, and I've been unapologetically hearing them, and seeing the spirits they come from, ever since.

But this is a book devoted to psychic children, and for all intents and purposes, with the exclusion of a whole lot of repetition, thus ended my psychic childhood. You can find the rest of my psychic life detailed in some of my other books. For now, to stay on point, I'll proudly move along to the next two psychic children in the family, my wonderful sons.

Paul and Chris

Yes, exactly as Grandma Ada predicted, I didn't become a nun after all. I had two sons who are as close to me as my own heart, and when they were very young we moved from Kansas City to California.

Paul Dufresne came first, an outgoing, very funny boy with a sense of humor identical to his mother's—to this day Paul and I can be doubled over with laughter in a corner of a room while everyone else stares at us wondering what on earth is so funny. From the time he was born he was as psychic as every other child, giggling and waving from his crib at spirits who stopped by his room to say hello, but he was neither very verbal about nor interested in the spirit world and his psychic gifts. He knew his Spirit Guide's name was Timothy but rarely talked about him, and when he was three years old he asked me in passing who the woman was who followed me around all the time, which of course was and is Francine. But from childhood to this very day, he was far more intent on pursuing his other gifts, which have culminated in his successful career in business and real estate. I'm so proud of him and so grateful for him, and I celebrate the passion with which he's pursued his own chart, independent and happy and fiercely devoted to and protective of his mother.

Chris Dufresne came along a few years later, as enchanted by his psychic gifts as his big brother wasn't. From the time he was an infant he could see and hear the spirit world around him, and it delighted him. You'll read in Chapter Three about his imaginary friend Joey, a ghost boy from whom Chris learned his first lesson in loving someone enough to let them go. But he also communicated regularly and openly with his Spirit Guide Charley even as a toddler, years younger than I was when I became aware of Francine, and unlike his mother, Chris found nothing frightening about Charley or any of the other spirits in his life. To this day, if there are too many people around for Chris's privacy comfort level, he'll do what he did as a child, and what I sometimes do as well, and disappear into the bathroom when he and his Spirit Guide need to talk.

One area in which Chris's psychic preferences and mine have always differed is that he loved astral projection, while I studiously avoid it. You'll read more about astral projection and astral travel in

Chapter Six, but briefly for now, astral projection is the very common process of the spirit taking temporary trips away from the body. It's especially popular with children, whose spirits are accustomed to their unobstructed gravity-free lives on the Other Side and are still adjusting to these silly, cumbersome, restricting bodies they've found themselves housed in. I'm sure I'd never have known how often Chris astrally projected himself if we hadn't had a shag carpet when he was a little boy. I can't count the number of times he'd be sitting beside me on the couch, quiet and peaceful, and it would suddenly occur to me that he was being a little too quiet and peaceful. I would look up and see tiny footprints in the shag carpet leading away from the couch as Chris, too playful to be contained, would be trotting merrily off to amuse himself elsewhere while his body dutifully stayed right there by my side. I'd say, "Chris, get back here!" and instantly feel his body become animated again, and he'd look up at me with the most innocent smile as if to say, "What are you talking about, Mom? I've been here the whole time."

Chris was aware of his chart and of his past lives from the beginning; they almost spilled out of him when he was able to start talking. He routinely said, "Mama, I came here to be with you," and thank God, he's lived his life accordingly. He would refer to our past lives together, particularly one in France. But his clearest memory of a past life came out one day when he was three years old. Due to his fascination with anything and everything to do with cowboys, I asked him, "Who were you before this?" As if he were telling me what he'd done the day before he replied, "I was a cowboy, and my horse was named Cinnamon. I was shot in the head in the street in front of a saloon, and my daughter held my head while I died." Chris was an incredibly bright boy, but believe me, that little story was beyond his vocabulary at the time, not to mention too detailed for him to have made up on the spur of the moment. I remember thinking how far beyond childhood I was before I became conscious of some of my past lives, and how delighted I was that his psychic gifts were so distinctly his own.

You'll be reading more about Chris, and about everyone else in this chapter, throughout this book. He's grown up to be a very successful professional psychic himself, as many of you already know. And of all the things I'm proud of about my two sons, nothing makes me more proud than the fact that they're the finest, most loving, most devoted fathers I've ever seen to the grandchildren they've blessed me with. Which leads to the next generation of psychic children in our family.

Jeffrey and Willy

Paul's son Jeffrey, with enough sweetness and sensitivity for any ten families, once looked up at me adoringly while curled up in my lap and said, "Grandma, when I grow up I want to be psychotic like you." It remains one of the most frequently used quotes among my sons and my staff when they get frustrated with me, and no one thinks it's funnier than I do.

Fortunately, Jeffrey doesn't have a psychotic bone in his body, and his psychic gifts haven't manifested themselves in any dramatic ways, with one exception: He is so psychically connected to his father that even as a small child he could always tell us with uncanny precision just exactly when Paul would be arriving home from work, no matter how many hours it varied from one day to the next.

Willy, who's Chris's son, is the one I wish I could bottle and send to every one of you who's depressed. He's happy, he's funny, and he's easygoing. He's also so conscious of the fact that we're all just visiting here from the Other Side that when the family is going through a crisis, he'll say without a hint of sadness or doom, "Bagdah (his and his sister's nickname for me), let's give it up and go back Home where we belong."

Like Jeffrey, Willy makes no issue of his psychic gifts, and they only spill out of him on an as-needed basis. You read in the first chapter about his momentary channeling of my father, whom he never met. And then there was the time when he was three years old, contentedly playing by himself in the family room. His mother Gina and I were on the sofa a few feet away, having one of those odd moments of contagious stupidity—I have no idea what we were talking about, but for no apparent reason we were both drawing a complete blank on the name of the most famous landmark in Paris. We couldn't think of it for the life of us, and we couldn't believe we couldn't think of it for the life of us. Willy seemed to be paying no attention to us while we stammered away, suddenly dumb as shovels, but finally, to put us out of either our misery or his, he glanced over just long enough to say, "Eiffel Tower, Bagdah." When we were done feeling like idiots, we then tried to fathom how and when, in his three short years on earth, he'd ever heard of the Eiffel Tower, let alone known it was a Paris landmark.

Willy's psychic gifts seem to be focusing themselves more acutely as he gets older, with no effort on his part or ours. Most conspicuously, he's the one we turn to when anything's missing around the house—he can tell us in an instant where to find it without breaking stride in whatever he happens to be busy with at the time. He recently announced that he wants to follow in my footsteps when he grows up. Like everyone else I'm very close to, I'm too emotionally invested to be accurately psychic about him. But I know that whatever he's charted for himself, he'll pursue it with a happy-go-lucky ease that never ceases to inspire me.

Angelia

Someone once described Chris's daughter Angelia as being "Sylvia's heart on two legs." It's a perfect description of our connection from the moment she was born, and there's a reason for that, far beyond her being my granddaughter: I knew the instant I saw her—psychically, spiritually, and absolutely—that Angelia was literally the reincarnation of my cherished Grandma Ada, back in a physical body, blessing me twice in one lifetime with that exquisite soul.

It's essential to remember in any case of a reincarnated spirit you recognize that, while every spirit retains its own essential identity throughout its eternal journey, every new incarnation means a new chart, new goals, and new challenges toward our spirits' ongoing growth. No reincarnation is a duplicate of the previous one, and no reincarnated spirit is a clone of whoever it was before. So as thrilling as it was to know that Grandma Ada was physically in my life again, I also knew she hadn't come back to be Grandma Ada; she'd come back to be Angelia, her own person with her own path to follow, and any expectations to the contrary on my part were going to be tough luck. And not a day goes by when I don't thank God that His wisdom supercedes mine, because I can't fathom the loss in my life if Angelia were anyone but exactly and uniquely who she is.

There was an unspoken universal agreement among our family—and that includes my staff, whom I count as family—that none of us would ever say a word to Angelia, or in her presence, about her being my reincarnated Grandma Ada, not even when she was an infant. Never trick yourself into believing that there's such a thing as a child who's too young to understand. The physical body and its conscious mind may be brand new, but the spirit mind that inhabits it is as timeless as eternity itself, and that spirit mind understands everything, from the moment you lay eyes on the newborn infant and long, long before. So putting the predisposed persona of Grandma Ada on baby Angelia was strictly off-limits from the very beginning.

But of course children being the psychic creatures they are, she didn't need us to tell her a thing. We were on a family trip to my hometown of Kansas City. Chris was driving as we toured the neighborhood where I grew up, and suddenly Angelia startled us all by yelling from the backseat, "Daddy, stop the car!" He did, with some screeching of brakes. She was excitedly pointing at a nearby storefront. "Bagdah, look!" she said. "Remember when I was big and you were little, and I used to carry you across the street to the grocery store right there?" I remembered perfectly how Grandma Ada had carried me across that street when I was a child, to a grocery store that by the time Angelia was pointing to it had become a hardware store. We were on that same trip when, giggling, she asked me, "Remember when I was Ada and I made you that nightgown with the ruffled collar, and you hated it?" (Not one of my finer childhood moments. Grandma Ada worked hard on that nightgown, but its high neck was itchy and tight and I refused to wear it.) My assistant Michael was rinsing out the office coffee pots one day when Angelia passed by and observed, "When I was Ada, I used to do that all the time," probably recalling the years when Grandma Ada ran a boardinghouse for which she was the sole one-woman cleaning crew.

There were visible signs of Grandma Ada in Angelia from the beginning. Some were subtle, like the way Angelia habitually brushed her hair back from her eyes, and a sharp, edgy wit beyond her years. Some were much more apparent: her love of writing; her kindness and compassion, particularly toward animals; her indignation over rude or cruel behavior; her gift for healing—I once saw Angelia hold a seemingly dying baby bird in her hands and, after several moments, a healthy baby bird fly away; and her fearless acceptance of the spirit world that has been part of her reality since the day she was born.

Angelia was very conscious of playing with her Angels as a child, and she was aware of Ariel, her Spirit Guide, although she never mentioned seeing her or actually hearing her as Chris and I hear our Guides, nor does she remember most of these experiences now. She did very clearly see Francine—she asked me when she was three years old who the woman with dark hair was who was standing behind me in the bathroom. And she had such an electrical force field around her that by simply walking into a room she could cause computers to crash, phones to offer nothing but static, and television sets to randomly change channels or simply shut off entirely until she left the room again. You'll read more about that force field, called kinetic energy, in Chapter Seven, and learn that Angelia wasn't the first in our family to experience that chaotic form of power over inanimate objects. In her case, it diminished as she got older and was nonexistent by the time she was eight or nine. We were all relieved. I'm not entirely sure she was. I saw her stifle a smile more than once when she was a little girl at the awareness that her simple presence could make funny things happen. It was never deliberate on her part, or intentionally destructive; it was just a child experiencing her power, and none of us blamed her a bit for the fact that she seemed to get a kick out of it.

There are stories of Angelia throughout this book, all of which I cherish and all of which are from her early childhood. As she approaches her teenage years she's becoming less and less interested in her psychic gifts and the attention that's always surrounded them. She's much more focused on her extraordinary gifts in writing and the performing arts, and on continuing to create her own unique, fascinating identity. Wherever her chart takes her, she can be sure that my heart, my pride, and my profound respect for the child she was and the young woman she's becoming will be right by her side.

CHAPTER THREE

Psychic Children:
Our Window to the
Spirit World

I t's a cliché and an inarguable fact that children are our future.

I wish it were equally common knowledge that children—because they're so innately psychic and still so fresh from the spirit world of the Other Side—are also living, breathing proof of our immortality. If we simply pay attention and listen, without fear, without prejudice, without interrupting or cutting them off out of our own confusion, without close-minded skepticism, without coming up with a hundred silly and completely illogical explanations for what comes out of their mouths, we'll find in children an end to our dread of death, and a brilliantly lit pathway to the eternity God promised us.

I'm not sure what it is about human nature that makes us so ready and willing to believe the darkest, most threatening doomsday rumors, no matter how ridiculous, but so hesitant to believe the most glorious, sacred affirmations, even when they're spelled out as simply and certainly as the fact that the sun rises in the east. I've been swearing to people for more than fifty years, and meaning it, that there is no such thing as the devil, there are no such things as curses, and the evil in this world is caused by the fact that evil is a strictly human quality, nonexistent in the spirit world. And yet there are those who are so accustomed to being afraid, and to the chaos of negativity, that they'll fiercely cling to those beliefs no matter what I say, or what the spirit world says through me.

Please don't misunderstand—I don't let anyone tell me what to believe or disbelieve, nor do I ever want you to. My beliefs are based on seventy years of research, intensive study, a lifetime of access to the spirit world that my God-given psychic gifts have provided, and, last but not least, an insistence that what I believe has to be logical to me. My first rule when it comes to my beliefs: think.

And that's what I urge you to do when it comes to your own beliefs, and most certainly to the psychic children around you and how you deal with them. Think. When a child sees and hears things you can't see or hear that are very real to them, think how you'd feel if someone was dismissive toward you about the things you see and hear that are very real to you. When a child volunteers factual information that they supposedly have no way of knowing, think about the only possible sources (or Source) of that information. When a child makes references to a past life experience on earth or on the Other Side, think how discouraged you'd be if you were talking about something that happened to you in your past and you were accused of making it up or being ridiculous. The more you think, and the more logic you apply to the wisdom children have to offer, the more apparent it will become that yes, those children have ageless spirits endowed by their Creator; yes, they possess knowledge that could only have come from Home; yes, the spirit world is as normal to them as this world is to you because they just came from there; and yes, that means that you, and all of us, can reliably believe in the divine, blissful truth that we do survive death and transcend to the familiar joy of the Other Side, exactly as God promised and children continue to prove.

Marissa's mother Lee passed away a year before Marissa's daughter Macy was born. As soon as Macy was old enough to talk she chattered away about all the nice visits she was regularly having with Grandma Lee. "I would say things like, 'I'm glad,' and 'Tell her hello,' but I honestly didn't pay much attention," Marissa wrote. "Frankly, I was on overload. I had taken guardianship of my seventeen-year-old brother, John, who was mildly disabled, and his 'acting out' behavior was getting out of control. I was nearing the end of my rope and wondering what I was going to do one day when Macy, who was then three years old, sat down on the floor in front of where I was sitting and announced, 'Grandma Lee said you have to get John back into therapy and she said if that doesn't work you need to send him back to live with his dad so that he can take care of him. It is not your responsibility.' I could hardly believe Macy's grandmother really had that conversation with her, but it made more sense than believing that speech came from a three year old!"

Lorraine shared the story of her four-year-old daughter Nicole, who talked a lot about the "nice, friendly man" who brought her cookies and tucked her in at night when she was scared. The man was "very high" (Nicole's synonym for tall) with light hair, and he "walks over the floor."

"I didn't pay much attention to any of this (after my husband and I made sure there was no way a strange man was getting into our house at night and bringing cookies to our daughter!) and never asked her about it. I figured she was just making up stories like children do.

"But then one morning she crawled into bed with me after my husband left for work and said, 'That nice Philip brought me crackers in the night when I was awake.' I couldn't believe my ears and asked her to tell me again who had brought her crackers. She repeated the name 'Philip' and my heart started pounding. My younger brother Philip had died six months before Nicole was born, and it's too long a story, but because of the circumstances of his death and how painful it was for all of us, my family and I never talked about him or even mentioned his name, least of all around Nicole. I said something like 'that's nice' and got up to go make breakfast like everything was normal, but I was really shaken up.

"It bothered me all day, and then I had an idea about how to prove to myself once and for all that Nicole picking the name Philip was a coincidence. I got out a box of family photographs from a shelf in the garage that I hadn't touched in years, and I invited Nicole to help me sort them. I didn't tell her who anyone was when we looked through them; I just started putting them in different piles. I almost fainted when she suddenly pointed to one of the pictures and happily yelled 'Philip!' She picked up a photograph of my brother Philip (blond hair, just like the 'light hair' she described, and just over six feet tall, or 'very high' as Nicole said he was) and showed it to me and said, 'This is my friend Philip.'

"I didn't know what to say, and I still don't. My husband thinks I coached her. I know I didn't, but for her to know there was any such person as Philip and then pick his photo out of what must have been more than a hundred random pictures seems impossible. Again, I've wracked my brain, and there's no way she could have had any of this knowledge. Can you please explain what's going on? It's really troubling me, Sylvia."

I wanted to share Marissa's and Lorraine's letters to illustrate the importance of thinking and applying logic when a child offers advice and information that seems impossibly beyond their reach. Marissa's exactly right; what three-year-old is going to take it upon herself to recommend therapy for a troubled family member, or offer her mother guidance about limiting her responsibilities? Isn't it far more logical that the child was simply doing exactly what she claimed—passing along a message from her concerned grandmother on the Other Side? Between those two alternatives, doesn't repeating a message make more sense to you?

And Lorraine personally witnessed a series of events that she's still trying to convince herself are impossible. Obviously, if they happened, they're not impossible. "There's no way she (the four-year-old daughter) could have had any of this knowledge." And yet, she has it, so there is a way.

I can't encourage you enough to exhaust every logical source of precociously insightful advice or accurate information a child possesses for what appears to be no reason. Ask friends, relatives, anyone and everyone who spends time with the child if they've even hinted at that advice or information. Check the access to all the photos in the house to see if the child could possibly have found and gone through them when you weren't looking. Honestly, be a detective. Leave no stone unturned. If you discover an earthly source of the child's knowledge, good for you, you've solved the mystery. If you don't, then the process of elimination leads to the only possible conclusion: The source of that knowledge is *un*earthly.

The word *unearthly* has become so widely misused that I'm sure it's part of the reason people associate it with some combination of fright and evil. Even *Webster's Dictionary* includes the words *weird*, *eerie, absurd,* and *ungodly* in its definition. But again, think. All *unearthly* really means is "not of earth" or "beyond earth." And beyond earth and its dimension lies the Other Side, our real Home, the most sacred, blessed, blissful, Godly place in His infinite creation. Believe me, in the cosmic scope of things, nowhere will we find more weirdness, eeriness, absurdity, and ungodliness than right here on earth. In my personal spiritual dictionary, *unearthly* is synonymous with "in the unconditional loving embrace of God."

So the more you think about it, Macy's passing along her grandmother's advice to Marissa, and of Lorraine's daughter Nicole knowing her deceased uncle Philip are not troubling at all, they're worthy of joyful celebration. They don't just validate that the grandmother and Philip are around, loving and comforting and involved in the family's current events. They also validate that their deaths really were just illusions, allowing glimpses through these innocent, guileless children of the eternal lives that God has promised us all.

It's very much worth noting, by the way, that Nicole noticed her uncle walking "over the floor." He was. Three feet over it, to be exact. One of the definitive signs of a visiting spirit is that they appear to be floating above ground level. That's simply because they're walking on *their* ground level, three feet above ours, in the higher dimension of the Other Side.

Another thing to remember about the spirit world of Home is that everyone knows each other. That's not a figure of speech; it's literally true. Which is why children will often know any number of details about family members and friends who passed away before the child was born—what they don't learn by chatting during spirit visits here, they learn by getting acquainted on the Other Side in that time between the passing of the loved one and the child's arrival on earth.

That's the case with Carl's daughter Olivia, who started talking about spirit visits when she was three but had also became acquainted with her deceased relatives at Home long before she came here.

"She doesn't just physically describe my favorite aunt, who died five years before Olivia was born. She talks accurately about how my aunt loved to knit, about my aunt's little black dog (a black pug who was my aunt's constant companion), and about how odd it was when my aunt's 'kitchen was in her parlor.' (My aunt spent her last years in an assisted living facility, and her dining table was in the living room.)

"One day she told me that my deceased father, her grandfather, came to visit 'when the moon and stars are out' and took her fishing. (My father was the most avid fisherman I've ever met.) She mentioned that he had black hair and no teeth. (My father had jet black hair, while the rest of the family is blond, and he didn't get dentures until after he left us.) And she said that my father liked to tell her about Akiba. I had no idea who or what that was, but after a lot of asking around I found out that Akiba was the name of my great-grandfather, whom I never got to meet.

"We let her talk as much as she wants when she wants, and we make sure never to give her the impression that there's something wrong with her, or that she's not 'normal.' And we've discovered that it's best not to ask her too many questions, because she'll answer maybe one or two of them and then she'll stop."

That's a wonderfully healthy approach to dealing with children when they're sharing information—listen with respect and interest, and never, ever make them feel as if there's anything wrong or abnormal with their having this information. As for asking questions, you'll find that different children respond in different ways. Some seem to feel as if they're being pushed to tell more than they're ready to, while others open up more with questions to guide them along. Experiment with both approaches and you'll find out quickly which the child you're dealing with prefers.

My granddaughter Angelia, for example, never appreciated being prodded about her psychic experiences when she was a little girl, and we all learned very early on to just let her volunteer information if and when she wanted to. Fortunately, she accepted being psychic as casually as she accepted having black hair and lavender blue eyes, so there was no self-consciousness to overcome and definitely no coaching required.

She was four or five years old when we went on a family trip to the South, and she and I decided that we wanted to see Elvis Presley's home Graceland one day, just the two of us. From the moment we left the wall where all Graceland visitors sign their names and started toward the house, Elvis Presley himself (in spirit form, of course—yes, forget the rumors, he really did die when and how the press said he did) began following us. I noticed him immediately but decided not to say a word to Angelia, so that I wouldn't be planting any suggestions in her mind or prodding her to say she saw something just to please me. He never left our sides for a moment during the tour, and only when it was over did she turn to me with her trademark nonchalance and say, "You know, Bagdah, Elvis was with us the whole time we were in there." I just nodded and acknowledged that I'd seen him too, and we left it at that.

An interesting footnote to that story, by the way: As Angelia and I stood at Elvis's grave site paying our respects, she announced quietly and with some concern, "That's not Elvis's body in there." I'm not advocating an exhumation, mind you, but if one is ever done

56

and it turns out that Angelia was right, it won't surprise me in the least.

Never doubt for a moment that spirits are absolute opportunists—they visit us all, but they virtually flock to those whom they know will see them, hear them, and welcome their presence without desperately trying to explain them away. And who better to flock to than children? Still tuned to the spirit world from which they've recently arrived, and devoid of the cynicism and amnesia that so often block spirit communication as they acclimate themselves to human life and grow into adulthood, psychic children are perfect hosts for visiting spirits. Those spirits are welcome, familiar, comforting reminders from the Home they've just left behind, and for which they—and we—will be Homesick throughout our lives on earth. It's a guarantee that spirits always, always have the best, most comforting intentions when they come to visit, whether it's to actively offer caretaking and companionship or simply to send messages through the receptive audience children provide that they're very much alive and well.

Jen shared a wonderful story about her son Darren. Four years before Darren was born, his brother Colin died of leukemia at the age of eight. It was such a devastating loss that Jen couldn't bring herself to keep photos of Colin on display around the house, and Darren was a God-sent joy in her life.

"When Darren was about three or four years old, I'd often find him alone in his room having meaningful, unintelligible chats with someone I couldn't see. I'd ask him who he was talking to and he'd always leave it at the simple reply, "Angel." I assumed he was either referring to a real Angel (I read Sylvia's books, so I know we all arrive on earth with Angels around us) or that he had a spirit friend named Angel he didn't feel like telling me about yet.

"One night he was watching the movie *Superman,* racing all over the house wearing a cape made from a blanket, leaping off the furniture pretending he could fly. At one point as he dashed past me he breathlessly commented, 'Boy, Angel sure does like Superman!' It jarred me, because his brother Colin had been such a Superman fan that we buried him in his cherished little Superman outfit.

"A few weeks later we went to visit Darren's grandmother, my husband's mother, in her new house. Darren wandered into her bedroom and promptly ran back out clutching a framed photo in his arms, excitedly screaming, 'Grandma, it's Angel! Where did you get a picture of Angel?!'

"Needless to say, it was a happy, healthy picture of his brother Colin. I've never referred to Colin as deceased since that day, or felt sad that Darren never knew him. What more proof could I ever ask for that Darren has known and played with Colin all his life?"

Then there's a story from Caroline, whose three-year-old son, Jimmy, insisted she didn't need to tuck him in and read bedtime stories to him because "the old lady likes to do it." The identity of the old lady became clear one day when Jimmy pointed to a snapshot in the family photo album of his long-deceased grandmother and announced, "That's her! The lady who reads to me!"

Jess's daughter Elizabeth sat down with her on the eve of her fourth birthday and, in amazing detail, told Jess a very long, involved children's story. "The more I listened," Jess wrote, "the more I realized that she was telling me a story my grandmother had told me a hundred times when I was growing up. My grandmother passed away ten years before Elizabeth was born, and I knew I had never told Elizabeth that story myself. When she finished I asked her where she'd heard it. With all the exasperation an almost-four-year-old can muster she said, 'I knew it since I was in your stomach, Mommy.' I asked everyone in my family if they had told Elizabeth the story, and sure enough, none of them had. Most of them didn't even know the story themselves. And my daughter hadn't started attending school yet, so I can eliminate that as a possibility too."

Is it too soon to urge you again to think? Not for a moment do I want you to get so focused on the strangeness of these stories, or on whether or not you believe them, that you miss the glorious validation of our spirits' survival in these beautiful accounts of children and their loving, helpful friends from Home. From what other possible source could these children get such accurate information? And how blessed are we to be given such obvious and easily accessible proof of eternity?

Of course, there are children who, in the process of making the sometimes overwhelming transition from the Other Side to earth, are more frightened than comforted by their encounters with spirits. And it's often an understandably difficult dilemma for the loved ones of a frightened child to deal with those fears in a productive way.

There are the well-intentioned parents who are simply trying to protect their child from something they themselves don't understand:

"My eight-year-old daughter, Bella, has been seeing what she calls 'ghosts' for about a year now, both in our house and at other places around town," writes Marti. "She is becoming extremely fearful about it and has trouble sleeping because the 'ghosts' are in her room. When she does get a good night's sleep, she's sure it's because the 'ghosts' are waiting in the bathroom. Occasionally when

I'm talking to her she'll suddenly stare past me like she's in a trance, and when I ask her why she explains that someone is standing there just looking at her. I look and don't see anyone, of course, and then she asks me why this keeps happening to her. I don't know what to tell her.

"Bella has also seen an old woman several times at my mother's house, not knowing that she's perfectly describing my grandmother, who lived in that house for a while and whom Bella never knew. She's becoming increasingly anxious and doesn't want to be alone. This is a big change from the little girl I knew a year ago.

"No one among our friends and most of our family believes that Bella is seeing things. They believe she's emotionally disturbed. I've seen and experienced things I can't explain too, including dark figures moving through the house, so I believe her, but no one believes my experiences either. I've only been having them for the past ten years or so, but poor Bella seems so young to start!

"I thought about calling our priest to come and bless our house, but since Bella sees her 'ghosts' at other places as well, it doesn't seem as if that would do any good. I would do anything to help her, but I have no idea where to start."

We'll be discussing ghosts, and the differences between ghosts and spirits, later in this chapter. But these are not ghosts that Bella is seeing. They're spirits from Home, from God, and it's not all that uncommon for them to appear as silhouettes, particularly to a child who's at an age when so many are finally becoming more of this earthly dimension than of the dimension of the spirit world they came from. As she becomes more tuned to earth than to the Other Side, her perception of the spirits she's routinely seen since she was born changes too. They become less distinct, less ordinary, and, sadly, less appropriate. Don't think for a moment that children aren't painfully aware when people around them whom they love and trust believe there's something wrong with them, that they're emotionally disturbed. Whether anything is said out loud in their presence or not, take it from someone who once was that child—they sense it, they feel the sting of it, and they can absolutely start to believe it. I'm willing to bet that Bella used to enjoy her spirit visitors, whether she talked about them or not, and that would explain the change in her in the past year from a happy child to a frightened one who's increasingly anxious and doesn't want to be alone. The more she's made to feel that seeing spirits means she's mentally ill, the harder she'll try to block them out, even though she's psychically sensitive enough to know that the spirits are still there. And of course they're still there. They've been enjoying their visits with her for eight years, and they're not eager for the day when their friend can't see or hear them anymore.

As I mentioned in Chapter Two, at night my bedroom when I was a child looked like Grand Central Station with so many spirits coming and going. And even with my Grandma Ada around to explain what was happening, I was afraid. So Grandma Ada took a practical approach to help me through the night while I was still struggling to understand who all these uninvited guests were: She gave me a flashlight to take to bed with me. It didn't make them go away, but it helped a lot to give me some sense of control, knowing I could shine a light on anything that was scaring me whenever I wanted and turn imagined monsters into the invariably kind, loving, friendly spirits they really were. A flashlight in bed. I can't recommend it enough.

On a far more spiritual note, I want you to start teaching children everything about the spirit world—that they were spirits before they came here, when they lived on the Other Side, and these are nothing more and nothing less than friends of theirs from Home who love them, coming to say hello and protect them and care for them, as good friends do. Teach them about their Spirit Guides and Angels, which you'll read about in Chapter Five. And above all, teach them that these beautiful spirits are visitors from God, and that God would never, ever send anyone or anything that would hurt them. Even ghosts, as you'll discover shortly, are not evil; they're just confused, but God's children nonetheless.

As for those who are uninformed and unknowledgeable enough to declare a child emotionally disturbed, or evil, or any other diminishing label they're unqualified to judge, insist that they keep their opinions to themselves from now on, and mean it. If you start to have justified concerns about your child's emotional health, please, by all means, seek out a fully credentialed, licensed professional, on referral from a trusted friend, family member, or physician. No one respects and appreciates the psychiatric community more than I do, believe me. But diagnoses from those who don't have a clue what they're talking about? Strictly off-limits. No exceptions.

Then there are the well-intentioned parents whose fear of the unknown inadvertently perpetuates fear in their psychic children instead of offering them the comfort, protection, and peace of mind they're trying to provide.

Charlotte wrote, "When my daughter Lucinda was three we moved into a new apartment, and Lucinda was terrified of her new bedroom to the point where she wouldn't sleep or even play in it. One night I was sitting on her bed with her trying to reassure her that there was nothing in her room to be frightened of when she suddenly looked at the window, began to cry, and kept saying, 'James! It's James!' Then her closet door opened and closed by itself, and I was even more scared than she was. I grabbed Lucinda and took her to my sister's house, where we stayed until we moved out of that apartment a week later."

I know it's hard to keep your emotions in check when you're startled by something and don't understand what it is. But sadly the lesson this child was taught by this experience was "When in doubt, run!" which won't serve her well either in her encounters with the spirit world or in life in general. I shudder to think how many more moves Charlotte has in her future, and how unintentionally she'll continue to teach her child to be afraid, unless she learns the truth about the utterly harmless phenomena Lucinda will continue to experience, and until she does a little research into her family tree. James is Lucinda's great-grandfather, whom Charlotte never knew or heard of, and he was simply coming to check on his beloved little ancestor and validating his presence by opening and closing the closet door.

Beth offered another very positive and inventive approach to helping a psychic child make peace with a spirit visitor who was frightening them at first. Beth's grandmother Patricia died a month before her daughter Chelsea was born. Beth and her grandmother were very close, and it was a devastating loss for Beth. One night Beth and her husband were awakened by the sound of Chelsea, age three, distinctly yelling the name "Patricia" over and over again at the top of her lungs. They ran to find Chelsea trembling in fear, telling them that "Patricia" had been sitting on the side of her bed.

"I assured her it was just a dream and stayed with her until she fell back to sleep, but I couldn't get over the fact that Chelsea had been calling out my grandmother's name. It seemed too strange to write off as a coincidence, and I couldn't imagine when Chelsea would have even heard anyone use the name 'Patricia'—even my husband exclusively called her 'Granny,' as I did. The next day I asked Chelsea about her dream, but she still seemed shaken up by it and didn't want to talk about it. Not sure what to believe, I decided to try to make something positive out of this even if it really was just a dream. So I told Chelsea I needed a favor from her: If Patricia came to visit again, would she please tell her something nice from me? It seemed to calm Chelsea down to have an 'assignment.'

"A few days later Chelsea woke up from a nap and came running to find me, not scared at all but excited and proud of herself. 'Mom, I told Patricia that you love her, and she said to tell you she loves you too, baby. And she says you and me look just like twins.'

"I couldn't have been more shocked. First of all, my grand-mother called me 'baby' from the day I was born until the day she died. No one else, including my husband, ever called me that. Second of all, most people think Chelsea looks like her father, until they see side-by-side pictures of Chelsea and me at her age, and they're amazed at how hard it is to tell us apart.

"There's not a doubt in my mind that my wonderful Granny is around my daughter and me, and I thank God for the comfort it brings me."

What a smart way to help distract a child from their fear and to validate the identity of a spirit visitor at the same time: Give the child a message to pass along and see what you get back. If nothing else, just as with Chelsea, it will make the child excited and proud to have successfully fulfilled a favor you asked of them. Good for you, Beth. And by the way, your grandmother knows why you couldn't be with her at the end, and she wants you to stop feeling guilty about it. As she says, the two of you always have been and always will be together, and no one can ever interfere with that.

Obviously I was lucky beyond measure to have Grandma Ada close by when I was a child to educate me as more and more spirit encounters came along. But it was easy for her, since she was so brilliantly psychic herself. I can't offer enough applause to those relatively un-psychic adults who, by accepting that what their children are seeing is real and God-sent, help them become less, not more, afraid.

Trudy wrote about her daughter Ashley, who began seeing Trudy's deceased father-in-law Barry around the house when she was three years old. "It was from Ashley's description that we recognized who she was seeing, and she confirmed it when she picked out my father-in-law in a group family photo taken at my wedding. She kept waking up during the night to find him standing at the foot of her bed watching her, and she was very afraid of him. My husband and I weren't sure how to handle it, but we knew my father-in-law and what a kind, loving man he was, and we decided to trust that that was his nature if not more so now that he'd moved on to the Other Side. So we told her that her Grandpa Barry was just coming to see her because he loves her and wants her to know him, but he doesn't mean to scare her. When she sees him and feels afraid, all she has to do is tell him he's scaring her and he'll go away. Well, she tried it and it worked! But even better than that, as time went on, now that she understood who he was and why he was there, she started inviting him to come back if he wanted to, but 'maybe just in the day sometimes.' Sure enough, she began getting glimpses of him around the house every once in a while 'in the day,' got used to his presence, and felt comforted by it. A few mornings ago she was happy to tell us that Grandpa Barry visited her in her room again while she slept and 'he's so nice!' No more fear. In fact, she feels very special that her grandfather comes 'all the way from heaven' just to see her."

If you ever find yourself wondering how to guide a child from fear of a visiting spirit to confidently welcoming it, I hope you'll reread Trudy's letter and follow her example.

This story from Justine made me laugh, and it's a great reminder that sometimes we're the ones who need knowledge more than our children do, and that just by asking a simple question or two we can clear up a whole lot of confusion. "We were having a small family gathering in my living room when my three-year-old daughter, Annie, suddenly became agitated, with a very worried little frown on her face. I asked her what was wrong and she pointed to the dining room and said there was a 'bad man' sitting at the table. We all looked and saw nothing, of course, and to calm her down we told her he was gone now. She looked again and turned back to us, annoyed as if we'd all lied to her, and said, 'He is not gone. He's right there at the table, and he's a bad man!' We thought maybe it would distract her if we had her concentrate on telling us what he looked like, and my sister got out a family album and asked her to point if she saw someone who looked like the 'bad man.' Within the first couple of minutes she gasped and pointed to a photo of my husband's deceased father and said, 'That's him! That's the bad man!' We couldn't imagine what she was talking about. No one ever met a kinder, sweeter man than my husband's father. But I have to admit it, for just about a second, because my child was so upset and so convinced it was him, I wondered if there was something about him I didn't know. In the meantime, my sister was busy telling Annie that no, her grandfather was a very nice man, and she asked what made her think he was bad. Annie's answer was, 'Because he's reading a book and he did not ask if he could first.' "

Yes, definitely, whenever possible, ask questions. Lifelong reputations could be riding on it.

And here's a story I love from Helen:

"My son Trenton has always had glimpses of what he thought were spirits, but the encounters were never long enough for him to be sure or identify who they were. Then came the tragic news that my younger brother Billy, who always led a very troubled life and had disappeared four years earlier, shortly before Trenton was born, had committed suicide in his girlfriend's apartment two thousand miles away. I hung up the phone from that call and was trying to collect myself for the calls I knew I needed to make to the rest of my family when Trenton came flying out of his room, terrified. I asked him what was wrong, and he said there was a man lying on his bed in black pants and a white shirt. The man smiled and told him, 'Take care of your mom, my friend,' and then he vanished.

"Well, there was only one person I could think of who always called people he cared about 'my friend,' and I found a picture of my brother Billy and showed it to my son. He immediately recognized him as the man on his bed. I hadn't even told Trenton the sad news about Billy yet, so he couldn't have come up with this story to try to comfort me, and there was nothing 'made up' about how terrified he was.

"I sat him down and explained that his uncle Billy had gone Home to live with Jesus, but he must have loved Trenton a lot to stop by on his way to say good-bye. (I know from reading your books that when someone commits suicide as a result of mental illnesses they can't help, they go straight to the Other Side just like the rest of us.) That seemed to calm Trenton down quite a bit. I wanted to call

Billy's girlfriend anyway, to offer my condolences, so I let Trenton sit with me while I called her and I finally asked her if she happened to know what Billy was wearing when he took his life. She did. It was his waiter uniform—black pants and a white shirt. I shared that with Trenton when I hung up and I could see that he was comforted and even proud that he'd known something he couldn't possibly have known and that such a special thing had happened to him. He now includes Uncle Billy in his prayers every night and tells him he can come visit again anytime."

Here's what I love most about that story: By some stretch of imagination, Trenton might have been able to randomly pick Billy out of a family photograph, possibly diminishing the credibility of the visit. But what wonderful validation of Billy's visit that Trenton was able to accurately describe what Billy was wearing when he died, a detail that no one else but Billy's girlfriend knew.

Again, knowledge is power, and never underestimate a child's ability to understand and accept what their spirit knows beyond all doubt from their life on the Other Side not that long ago: that visits from Home, no matter how startling they might be at first, are treasures from God to be cherished and celebrated.

In the end, isn't that healthier, more comforting, and far more honest than simply grabbing your child, running out of your house in a panic, and moving? Just think, if my family had taken that approach when I was a child, we would never have lived in the same house two nights in a row.

And to clear up a very common issue that appeared in many letters and that I've been through myself:

"My son Scotty was three years old when his father died. His father used to visit him regularly 'from heaven' and they would play and have long talks that left no doubt in my mind that these visits were real. (I admit I was a little envious, since I only saw him once, for a few seconds.) Scotty is almost seven now, and he hasn't seen his father for quite a while. He's sad that his father seems to have stopped coming. I am too. But I don't know what to tell him. Has his father really stopped coming, or has Scotty just 'outgrown' his ability to see him?"

I used to see my beloved Daddy fairly frequently in the first years after he passed away too, but his appearances became less and less frequent as time went on. I asked my Spirit Guide Francine what was happening—it started to upset me, frankly, that I could see everyone else's deceased loved ones but I'd stopped being able to see the loved one I missed so terribly.

According to Francine, just as we get more and more acclimated to the earth's dimension the longer we're here, we also get more and more reacclimated to the dimension of the Other Side the longer we've been back Home again, and it becomes harder and harder to physically make the vibrational transition from there to here. Francine has described it as being a bit like a deep-sea diver who surfaces too quickly and ends up with what divers call the bends. I've often used the analogy of the blades of an electric fan to illustrate the differences in frequency. At a fan's slowest speed, the blades are easily seen and easily distinguished from each other, analogous to our vibrational speed as humans. At medium speed, the blades are still visible but begin to blur and become harder to distinguish, which relates to ghosts who are caught between our dimension and the dimension of Home. At their highest speed, the blades rotate so quickly that they seem to become invisible, just as the Other Side, only three feet above our ground level, is a dimension whose frequency is so much higher and faster than earth's that it seems invisible to us. And yet it's every bit as real as the blades of that fan that we know perfectly well are there. So a spirit traveling from that fastest speed to the slowest speed understandably needs more and more concentration and control the longer they're accustomed to that higher vibrational level.

If and when the actual sightings of loved ones fade away, don't believe for a moment that they're not around you anymore. They'll still give you signs if you, and your child, know what to look for. Spirits find electrical power to be a very helpful conductor to which they can attach their energy, so watch for clocks and appliances that might start behaving strangely, television sets that turn themselves on and off or channel surf with no help from you, phones that ring with no one on the other end, or lights that flicker far longer than a burned-out bulb could cause. And by all means, having nothing to do with electricity, watch for the sudden appearance of coins in places they have no reason to be. Why spirits love to manipulate coins I have no idea, since they obviously have no need for money themselves. But make a game with your child of looking for coins, either single ones or clusters of them, where they don't belong. And when you find them, teach your child to smile and say thank you to the loved one they've been missing, who's simply doing what the spirit world yearns for when it comes to us on earth: letting us know that they're very much with us, that they're alive and well, and that, through God's grace, we can count on surviving death just like they did.

Ghosts

My son Chris was four years old when he started playing with and talking to what would commonly be called his "imaginary friend" Joey. He shared his food and toys with Joey, he made room for Joey on the couch when he watched TV, and he routinely asked me to tuck both him and Joey into bed at night.

The fact that no one but Chris could see or hear Joey didn't surprise me, nor did it trick me into believing for a moment that Joey was imaginary. I've never met a child whose consistent, ongoing imaginary friend didn't turn out to be a very real visitor from another dimension. If I can't always see or hear them, it's only because I've also never met a psychic adult or child whose perception includes each and every resident of the other dimensions that constantly interact with us here on earth. And thank God for that. I see quite enough of them. I'm sure I would lose what's left of my sanity if I could see them all.

So I was perfectly happy to welcome my child's very real imaginary friend into my home. Because Chris has always been very private, sharing what he considers to be personal information when he's good and ready and not before, I didn't ask questions about Joey; I just waited patiently for Chris to tell me about him at his own pace.

And I can honestly say I didn't see it coming when one day Chris sadly announced, "Mama, Joey's all burned."

For the millionth time, I was so grateful at that moment for my lifetime of experiences and knowledge that allowed me to recognize exactly what was happening and how to address it with my sweet, sensitive, empathetic little boy. I pulled him into my lap and put my arms around him as I explained it to him.

"Sweetheart," I said, "that means that Joey is very sad and confused, and he needs our help. Do you know why?"

Chris shook his head.

"Because his life on earth ended in a fire, but he hasn't gone Home to God yet. He thinks he still belongs here, and he doesn't understand where his family and friends have gone. He's a ghost, Chris. He's trapped here, and we need to tell him he's dead so he'll find the Light that will lead him to the Other Side where God and the Angels and all those people who love him are waiting for him."

"I'll miss him," Chris said, starting to cry.

"I know you will," I told him. "But he can come back to visit you when he's a spirit, and he'll be so happy and he won't be burned anymore because God's perfect Light will heal him."

Chris thought about that, and a few moments later he stopped crying and smiled a little. "Then let's help him go Home, Mama," was all he said.

I was so proud of my young son for being unselfish enough to encourage his friend to leave, and after prayers, a few talks with Joey, and some help from Francine and from Joey's Spirit Guide, we successfully sent him through that glorious Light into God's loving arms on the Other Side.

A woman named Elizabeth shared a similar story of her four-year-old daughter, Cara, but with a question I've been asked over and over and over again by parents whose children have a friend that only the children can see:

"My daughter Cara has an invisible best friend named Jamie. She tells me that Jamie is a little girl who lives in the street and wears her hair over one eye because she was run over by a car. Cara draws pictures of Jamie, and I can hear her in her room at night talking to Jamie. I never ask Cara about Jamie. We only talk about her when Cara brings her up. But I can't help but wonder, is Jamie evil? Is Cara making all this up? I don't understand why it's happening, because my daughter is really a very happy child who in every other way seems so normal."

Well, for all the reasons we discussed in the first chapter, and earlier in this one, it's the most normal, natural thing in the world for children to see and hear beings from other dimensions. And it's the most normal, natural thing in the world for those beings to seek out children to communicate with, appreciating that children, psychic and guileless as they are, will receive them openly and without judgment.

It's also imperative to understand who those beings are and the differences between them, not only for your own peace of mind but so you can explain what's happening to the children in your life as well. As the stories of my son Chris and his imaginary friend Joey, and Cara and her invisible friend Jamie illustrate, it's really very easy to tell if a being your child is interacting with is a ghost as opposed to a spirit from the Other Side. If that being is injured, scarred, physically challenged, impaired in any way, unhappy, angry, aggressive, or even slightly unkind, it's a ghost, earthbound, caught between dimensions, and it needs to be told, essentially, "You're dead. Go Home." It's simple logic: The Other Side is perfect bliss, where no pain or impairment or emotional turbulence exists. The presence of any of those earthly imperfections is a dead giveaway (if you'll forgive the expression) that the being in question hasn't found its way Home yet.

And that's exactly what ghosts are: spirits who've left their bodies when their bodies stopped functioning and, by leaving their bodies, left the dimension on earth. But for reasons of their own—never by God's choice—they've turned away from or not seen the tunnel and the Light of the Other Side, which means that they're not part of that dimension yet either. Instead, they're literally neither here nor there, in a midrange dimension that typically makes them more visible and audible than fully transcended spirits.

Understandably, because they haven't experienced the tunnel and the trip Home, all ghosts share one universal tragic characteristic: They don't have the slightest idea that they're dead, which makes it hard to feel anything but sympathy for their equally universal confusion. Imagine waking up tomorrow thinking everything's just like it was yesterday, but as the hours and days and weeks and years wear on you discover that only a handful of people seem to be able to see or hear you—and many of them do nothing but scream at the sight or sound of you. Family and friends act as if you don't exist. Strangers arrive at your home with all their furniture and belongings and nonchalantly set up housekeeping without so much as acknowledging your presence, let alone explaining themselves. Someone has taken your place at work and even disposed of your personal items, assuming you can get to your job at all, since your car keys seem to slip right through your hands, and for no apparent reason you're not even solid enough to dial your phone anymore. No wonder ghosts are often cranky and sad and more than a little deranged. You would be too, if your whole world changed that suddenly and that radically without your having a clue as to what might have caused it.

A nine-year-old boy named Greg gave a perfect description of this lonely dimension in which ghosts live, and on which we unknowingly intrude, when he and his family moved into a two-story house in northern Minnesota. Greg's parents began feeling odd sensations of foreboding, and of being watched, from their first day in their new home, but they never discussed their discomfort with their son, eager for him to be comfortable and not wanting to plant fears in his mind. But one day he announced, "You know, there are four ghosts in this house."

His mother, Julia, tried not to sound startled and asked if he knew who they were.

"It's a mother, a father, and two children. They didn't have enough heat, and they froze to death." Greg then went on to add, "I can see their house on top of this one but with their stuff."

I couldn't have put it better myself.

The reasons for ghosts turning away from the Light and refusing to accept their death are as varied as the ghosts themselves. Some stay behind out of a confused loyalty to or passion for a loved one, a specific house or location, or a job to which they devoted their lives and believe still exists. (Their confusion is always compounded by the fact that, trapped between dimensions as they are, they're also trapped in their own time and space warp, having no conscious awareness that often decades or even centuries have passed and the physical world they're occupying has completely changed.) Others stay behind out of fear of an impossibility: That they've too completely disappointed God to be welcomed into the embrace of His unconditional love. Or, as a seven-year-old named Marilyn explained to her parents about a ghost friend of hers, "He doesn't want to go into the Light because he's afraid of a word that starts with *h*." (Marilyn's mother's letter explained that *hell* is an unacceptable word in their house.) And for the record, no matter how many screenwriters and authors create the opposite impression, only a handful of ghosts stay behind in search of revenge.

But even when it comes to vengeful ghosts, I want to stress something that you can take to heart and most certainly use to assure the children in your life who are interacting with ghosts. I've been averaging ten to twenty clients a day for more than a half century, and I've investigated more hauntings than I can begin to count. Despite all the movies, books, and tabloid stories to the contrary, not once have I ever found a legitimate case of a ghost—even a vengeful one—who's actually caused physical harm to anyone. Not once. The closest I've come is clients who hurt themselves out of panic over a supernatural encounter. So please, please don't add to any fear a child might be experiencing by implying that a ghost might attack them. It's just not true.

There are certainly ghosts who, in their sometimes aggressive confusion, perceive the living people around them to be intruders and potentially threatening, and they'll be as disruptive as their limited powers allow in an effort to scare us intruders away and have their space to themselves again. They'll run and crash around the house, they'll slam doors and cupboards, they'll throw piles of papers off a desk in a room where there's not even the slightest breeze, they'll toss pictures off of walls and empty the contents of drawers and cabinets into the middle of the floor, they'll literally go bump in the night. Unnerving and scary as all this turbulence can be, remember, ghosts are not trying to actually injure anyone. Many of them just want us gone.

But just as often, particularly with ghost children appearing to living children, they can be playful, simply wanting to make friends and find some comfort in a world that no longer makes sense to them.

Jackie tells the story of her five-year-old son, Matthew, who sud-

denly began giggling uncontrollably while sitting alone at the breakfast table one morning. "I looked over to see what was so funny, but
his eyes were focused on nothing but the empty chair across from
him," Jackie wrote. "I asked what he was giggling about and he just
shrugged. It took a couple more times of asking before he finally
pointed at the empty chair and said, 'He's making me laugh.' I
couldn't imagine what game he was playing with me. Finally I
walked over to the empty chair, pulled it away from the table, and
passed my hand over the seat. Matthew got very upset because I
scared 'the boy' away. I sat down with him and asked him what 'the
boy' looked like, and he described a child with a severe facial disfig-
urement, who'd been playfully making faces at him while he ate his
breakfast. I wrote it off to Matthew's vivid imagination until about a
year later, when I myself caught a brief glimpse of a little boy with a
severely disfigured face who appeared for just an instant or two in
our dining room."

I'll probably say this a million times throughout this book, but
when children tell you stories, no matter how far-fetched they might
sound, you'll do yourself and them a huge favor by eliminating the
word *imagination* from your vocabulary. You could be dismissing a
treasure trove of valuable information by assuming that because
they're just children, they can't possibly see, hear, and know things
that are beyond us adults.

Nell tells a wonderful and very typical story about her son
Danny. The family had been catching movements throughout the
house out of the corners of their eyes from the moment they moved
into their new home. At around that same time three-year-old
Danny began talking about Buddy, his new friend in the house that
no one but he could see.

"He would caution me not to shut the door on Buddy when we were leaving the house or casually mention that he'd just been playing with Buddy, and Buddy became a constant 'pretend' presence in the family to everyone but Danny. This went on for about two years, during which I often heard the sound of someone running around downstairs and the front door opening and closing in the middle of the night while we were all upstairs in bed.

"One night while I was sleeping Danny climbed up into bed with me—our bed sits very high off the floor. I must have been vaguely aware of him, because I woke up with the thought that I'd better pull Danny closer to me so he wouldn't fall off the bed. When I turned to reach for Danny, who was sound asleep, I saw a small boy peeking up over the mattress at me. It was just a smoky apparition at first, but as it took shape I distinctly saw the little face and knew this child was genuinely, deliberately peeking at me, as in a playful, silly game of peek-a-boo. I threw my arms around my son and held him tight, and I made myself look around the room to determine whether I was awake or asleep. There was no doubt about it that I was awake, and when I looked back to the edge of the mattress where the little boy had been, he was gone.

"The next morning I asked my son if he knew where Buddy lived. 'He lives under your bed, Mommy,' he said.

"It was about a week later when Danny came downstairs looking very sad, and I asked him what was wrong.

" 'I don't have Buddy anymore,' he told me.

" 'Why? Where did he go?'

"Danny replied, 'He went far, far away to be with his parents.'

"None of us ever caught movements out of the corners of our eyes again, and the sounds of running and the front door opening and closing stopped that day.

"I'm one hundred percent sure of what I saw that night in my bedroom, and I'm convinced that Buddy was much more than the imaginary playmate my husband and I thought he was at first."

This was a ghost child named Richard Gibson or Gibbons, by the way. Danny heard him say he wanted to be his buddy and mistook that to be his name. Danny's family can validate this if they'll look into a history of the property—not the house itself, but the property, which has been there for a millennium or two. Richard Gibson or Gibbons died during childhood of an accidental drowning in the creek that once formed the boundary between that property and the acreage adjacent to it. As often happens with ghosts, loved ones on the Other Side—in this case, Richard's parents—came to retrieve this playful little earthbound boy and take him Home, and he'll be back in spirit form to visit Danny soon.

I can't urge you enough to research and try to validate as much information as you can glean from a child's encounters with ghosts. You'll be shocked at how accurate most children are about their imaginary playmates when you insist on looking into it and how ultimately comforting it will be to you and to the child to confirm that the entities they're seeing and hearing are real and traceable. I've had clients reject the idea of researching the ghosts their children experience, with the argument that they don't feel it's healthy to indulge childhood fantasies. My only response to that is, which would you rather be: stubborn, or smarter than you are now?

One of the luxuries of researching ghost sightings is that, unlike transcended spirits, who can move freely through sheer thought projection and even bilocate (be in two places at once), ghosts are literally earthbound and tend to stay in a location or area that's familiar to them. Which also means that if a child is sensitive to any ghosts who might be in and around their home, they're likely to be sensitive

to other ghosts no matter where they are. It's easy to jump to the er-
roneous conclusion that some pesky ghost is following your child
around. But no—different locations, different ghosts, and children
understand the difference if you listen closely enough.

For the first few years of her life Angelia was aware of a ghost in
my house, a Native American woman who was buried on this land
hundreds of years ago. Angelia wasn't afraid of her, just aware, and
more aware of her than I was, I might add. When Eya (Angelia's
nickname) was six years old, Lindsay, my friend and writing partner,
came to spend a few days with me while we worked on our first book
together, *The Other Side and Back*. Shortly after Lindsay arrived, Angelia pulled her aside for a private talk. Eya wasn't pronouncing her
r's yet, so the conversation went like this:

"What woom are you staying in?" Angelia asked.

"The one right up the hall from yours," Lindsay told her.

"You know, thewe's a ghost in that woom," Angelia said. "She's an
Indian."

Lindsay's been around the spiritual block enough to feign concern rather than actually feeling it. "Will she hurt me?" she asked.

Angelia gave one of her trademark "boy, are you stupid" eye rolls
and replied with an exasperated, "She's a *ghost*, Lindsay."

Lindsay promised that if she woke up during the night and a
ghost in her room was scaring her, she would walk straight up the
hall and get Angelia to tell the Indian woman to go away. They gig-
gled for a minute or two about the stern speech Angelia would give
the Indian woman with her little hands on her little hips, but suddenly Eya stopped laughing, grew very intent, and leaned close to
Lindsay's face to whisper, "Sewiously, Lindsay, thewe is a ghost."

To this day Lindsay and I still work the word "sewiously" into our conversations as often as possible. As for the Indian woman, Angelia informed me several months later that she had successfully sent her Home, and she never mentioned her again.

I've taken Angelia on countless trips with me, before and since her experience with the ghost in my house, and we've had our share of encounters. I told you earlier about Elvis's spirit following us around Graceland without either of us mentioning it until we were outside the house again. But it was at the Britannia Hotel in Greece where we had our first spontaneous ghost sighting together.

We were in the ladies' room off the lobby, waiting for our car to pick us up. I was turning away from the sink as Angelia emerged from a stall, so we were facing each other about four or five feet apart. With no warning whatsoever the white wispy form of a woman appeared out of nowhere, passed right between us, and vanished again. There was no need to ask each other, "Did you see that?" Our identical facial expressions—eyes as big as saucers, mouths hanging open—said it all, and we couldn't help but laugh at how suddenly a passing ghost had magically transformed us into shocked, silent mirror images of each other. There was nothing else to this sighting other than the obvious fact that we spontaneously validated each other's fleeting but very real experience.

A similar event occurred at the Norfolk Hotel in Kenya. Eya and I emerged from our room to see a distinct filmy being, definitely a woman again, glide past us down the hallway and into the nearby ballroom. Angelia, fearless as always, hurried after her and was crestfallen to discover that once the woman had arrived in the ballroom she'd vanished and was nowhere to be found.

In both of those cases, and in my own personal spirit world encounters in almost every other country on earth, my questions to the

81

locals about resident ghosts were greeted with shrugs of total acceptance and variations of "Oh, yes, our ghost(s). Aren't they wonderful? We're so blessed to have them."

It would be a compassionate, sacred gift to our children if we
could be as educated, accepting, and respectful of the vast population in those God-given dimensions beyond our own as the other
supposedly less civilized nations with whom we share this planet.

If you do find yourself living with one or more ghosts, even if
they seem friendly, please be compassionate and respectful but remember that they don't belong here and, in their confusion, they're
depriving themselves of the joyful, sacred peace of the Other Side.

Learn, and teach your children, to say to any ghosts you or they
might encounter, "This lifetime has ended for you. You're free to go
to the Other Side now, where God and your loved ones are waiting
to welcome you Home." You may not succeed in sending them
Home the first, second, or even tenth time you try. Don't forget,
you're dealing with a confused being who has yet to even accept the
fact that they're dead. But be patient and diligent and sooner or later
you and your child are likely to share the same gratifying act of kindness my son Chris and I shared with his little ghost friend Joey when
Chris was a child: Helping an earthbound spirit find its way into
God's arms again where it belongs.

Imprints

Less common than spirits and ghosts but with every bit as dramatic an impact on psychically sensitive children is a phenomenon
called an imprint.

An imprint is a specific site at which a very dramatic event or series of events has occurred and had such an intense impact that the imagery and emotions from those events have literally become imprinted on the land and the atmosphere where they took place. Not only do the intensely concentrated images and emotions continue feeding on themselves, but everyone who experiences and reacts to an imprint contributes their own energy to it and helps perpetuate it.

I learned the hard way about imprints, never having heard of them until I was well into my forties and found myself in the midst of one on a stretch of Highway 152 in Northern California called Pacheco Pass. My then-husband, Dal, was driving, and I was staring idly out the passenger window when suddenly I felt as if I'd been hurled into an abyss of frantic, terrifying anguish so paralyzing that I truly believed I'd lost my mind and soul. There were deafening sounds of torture and death. There were hideous images of children trapped in burning covered wagons, Spanish soldiers torching hanging corpses, Indians circling wildly on horseback while others were being beaten, a melting pot of races locked in mortal combat, flames consuming small primitive shacks. The smell of gunpowder and burning flesh assaulted me, and I couldn't breathe, or see through what felt like a fire in my eyes. Time stood still. I became disoriented, and for days afterward I was completely saturated with a deep depression, the same feeling of hollow, hopeless doom that had become part of the air itself at Pacheco Pass.

Subsequent research led to the discovery that Pacheco Pass was part of the violently tragic "Trail of Tears" that locked the Native Americans, the Spanish, the Mexicans, and the American settlers into years of war atrocities, all consistent with what I'd seen and felt in the throes of that imprint. It also led to the discovery that hundreds of people before me had reported inexplicable occurrences at Pacheco Pass, from sudden panic and feelings of impending death to actually gaining or losing time. The California Highway Patrol confirmed that incidents of felony road rage, fatal car accidents, and even suicides were higher through Pacheco Pass than anywhere else in their jurisdiction.

It was that experience that made me determined to get to the bottom of what could cause such a stunning array of reactions and incidents, which is what led to my intensive study and exploration of those vortexes of concentrated energy called imprints.

The deep sense of grief and loss and heroism that engulfs you when you visit Ground Zero in New York are caused by its imprint. The overwhelming fear, sadness, violence, and occasional images of cannons, rifles, and dying soldiers so many have experienced when visiting Gettysburg or Normandy are caused by their imprints. The reverent awe of God's miracles that penetrates to the souls of those who visit Lourdes is caused by its imprint. And every person who visits an imprint and is deeply affected by it feeds even more energy into its already powerful magnitude.

One of the most amazing facts about imprints is that they easily can be mistaken for hauntings, which is why I wanted to clarify them in this discussion of children and the spirit world. Both imprints and hauntings can evoke very dramatic emotions and the illusion of very real sensory experiences. Both imprints and hauntings can include undeniable humanlike images. The crucial difference is that the beings in an imprint are not earthbound, nor are they even alive in the setting of the imprint. The actual participants in the events that create imprints have long since transcended to the Other Side. Their remaining images, like the heightened sensory and emotional drama around them, are like three-dimensional holo-grams, permanent illusions in a never-ending, never-changing movie scene. But one significant difference between ghosts and imprint images: An imprint image will never interact with or even notice the humans around them, any more than a hologram would.

I got a handful of letters from understandably frightened victims of imprints, every one of whom believed there were demons and evil involved. If you never listen to another word I tell you, please, please listen to this: *There are no demons, and the only evil you ever need to worry about exists right here on earth, in human beings, not in the worlds of spirits and ghosts!* But having experienced the disorienta-tion, the overwhelming doomed hopelessness, and the sensory as-saults of an imprint myself, I can understand the confusion.

To give you just one example:

"I was four years old, in my bed, when a demonic figure ap-peared in my room and told me to come with him," Kate wrote. "A moment later more of these figures started to arrive. I tried to run for my bedroom door, but the floor opened up in front of me. Suddenly I felt this searing heat surrounding me, and I started screaming, 'Fire!' My bedroom door was always open, but that night in the middle of this horror it was closed and locked. My par-ents had to break down the door to get to me, and when they got into my room they felt the terrible heat too, but there was no fire to put out. My mom was sure it was a nightmare, and I might have believed her if they hadn't thought there was a fire just like I did when they saw how boiling hot it was in my room in the middle of winter."

This is a classic case of a small, very isolated imprint. If the family will check the history of the property, they'll find that in the early 1900s a nursing home stood on that land, and all its residents and many of the neighbors died in a cataclysmic fire. The figures who appeared were essentially holograms of the firemen, trapped in the repeating time warp of the imprint. (The first figure, who said, "Come with me," wasn't interacting with the child; he was just repeating his lines from all those years ago when he was trying to rescue the nursing home residents.) The floor appeared to fall away just as it actually had in the fire. The child herself, in her panic, closed and locked the door without realizing it, trying to keep herself safe from the seemingly demonic figures who seemed to be approaching her. But the real tip-off is the vortex of sudden searing heat in a room in which there's no fire at all, on a site where a fire once caused so much personal devastation that its imprint still exists and has been fed for generations by terrified children and their equally frightened parents for whom the real danger passed more than a hundred years ago.

You'd think that as a psychic, I'd be able to sense an imprint a mile away, especially when it comes to my own family, but I guess in a way it makes sense, especially in this book, that my child spotted one in our home before I did.

My only excuse is that I was a young wife and mother, excited about moving into my first house with my very own family—my husband, our son Paul, and our German shepherd, Thor. My fantasies of the cozy little nest I was going to create vanished into thin air when Paul promptly made it clear that he had no intention of sleeping in what I thought was the most perfect bedroom any little boy could ask for. He was too young to talk, so instead he screamed, he cried, he wrapped himself around my leg, he pointed frantically at things I couldn't see, he did everything but run away from home to keep me from dragging him into that room. And in case Paul didn't convince me that something was wrong with that room, Thor was right beside him, growling into the open doorway, teeth bared, hair on his back standing straight up as if it were electrified. In my defense, I did notice that the room was very cold. I thought I'd solve that by opening the floor heating vent. You guessed it—it was already open, but the room was at least twenty degrees colder than the rest of the house. And cold spots are common signs of energy vortexes, which is exactly what imprints are.

A lot of phone calls and research on the property our new little house occupied revealed the fact that Paul's room sat directly on top of an Indian burial ground hundreds of years old. It wasn't the confused, earthbound ghosts of those Indians who inhabited his room. It was an imprint of the profound, grief-stricken mourning that took place on that land so long ago, compounded by the subsequent understandable outrage of the Indians' descendents when a site so sacred to them was callously claimed and desecrated by land developers.

Once I understood what was going on in Paul's room, I never insisted that he or Thor spend a single moment in it. For the record, it wasn't long before the house in general became too psychically disruptive for any of us to tolerate, and we moved out far sooner than we'd intended. I've never met a ghost I wouldn't take on, but there's no defeating the powerful emotional vortex of an imprint.

Tulpa

"I know you don't believe in demons and devils," Eva wrote, "so I hope you can explain to me what I saw staring in at me through

87

my mother's bedroom window when I was six years old. I'm thirty-four now, and it still haunts me. I guess I should explain that my mother was a difficult woman. She saw evil in everything, in a self-righteous, judgmental, hell-fire-and-brimstone way. I grew up seeing spirits and ghosts all the time, but I would never have dared to mention it to her or she probably would have slapped me and had her pastor do an exorcism on me or something. She believed in curses, she believed in her Ouija board, and she believed in a real living, breathing devil as much as she claimed to believe in God. So one day I was in her room looking for something she asked me to bring her, and I looked out her second story window and was face to face with a huge awful creature. It had big red eyes that never blinked. Its nose was human looking, but it had fangs instead of teeth that I could see because its mouth was open and it was drooling. Its skin was gray and thin like parchment paper so that I could see its veins underneath, and even through a closed window I could hear that its breathing was loud and sounded like it was on respirator tubes. This thing and I both stayed perfectly still for what I'm sure was two or three minutes, just staring at each other, and I knew that whatever it was, it wanted me dead. Finally I got over my shock enough to scream and run out of the room. When I worked up the courage to peek back in at the window again, it was gone. I went outside to look a few minutes later, and there were no footprints or anything where it would have been standing. My mother asked what I was screaming about and I told her 'nothing.' Maybe I didn't want to give her the satisfaction of being right about the devil, I don't know. I never told her or anyone else about what I saw until now. I'm a good person who loves God and lives a kind, compassionate life, but I didn't imagine that creature outside my mother's window, and it would give me such peace of mind to know—if it wasn't the devil, what was it? God bless you for your help."

No. It wasn't the devil. It was a creature created by your mother, Eva, a perfect illustration of how powerful our minds really are, and how true it really is that we create what we fear. What you saw outside that window was a phenomenon called a tulpa.

A tulpa is a being that originates in the mind and exists nowhere else but there until, through obsessive belief and constant visualization, becomes an actual tangible physical reality with a life of its own, and then gathers strength as the belief in its existence intensifies. A tulpa is one of the most obscure, fascinating, and misunderstood beings your child (or you) might ever encounter, and can also be one of the hardest to get rid of.

To fully understand what a tulpa is, you have to know the story of a woman named Alexandra David-Neel. She was born in Paris in 1868 and was far ahead of her time as a scholar, researcher, adventurer, and writer. She frequently traveled throughout Asia to explore and experience everything from Eastern mysticism to mind-over-matter techniques to the teachings of Buddha to Tibetan spirituality and culture.

The Tibetans introduced her to the tulpa concept, their belief that you could manifest an actual entity into physical existence by mentally conceiving it, and she was so enthralled that she decided to experiment with the discipline of creating one herself. She chose to mentally conceive a portly, friendly, harmless little monk. She then began the intense prescribed routine of visualization and focused concentration, and eventually, to her amazement, she was able to see her little monk not just as her own personal mental creation but as a living physical being, separate from herself, as real as the rest of the world around her. The more she visualized him in her mind, the more solid and visible he became and, to her shock, the less control she had over him. He started making appearances at his own convenience rather than hers, and within a few weeks, people who knew nothing about her tulpa experiment began seeing him too.

What alarmed her most, though, was that the longer her little monk existed independent of her, the more he began developing his own persona having nothing to do with the one she'd visualized for him. He began to evolve into a stronger, more slender version of himself, while his personality change from pleasant and endearing to sullen, dark, menacing, and completely unpredictable. David-Neel became frightened of him and knew she had to destroy this increasingly dangerous being she'd created but could no longer control. She also knew that the only way she could destroy him was by absorbing him back into her mind where he came from. By then the monk tulpa felt absolutely entitled to exist and put up a fierce fight against his creator's efforts to eliminate him. It took over a month of the same intense concentration that manifested him for her to destroy him. The process was so debilitating that David-Neel's health was almost destroyed right along with the sinister little creature she'd brought into this world.

Tulpa, then, are powerful projected thoughts and emotions that become telescoped into physical forms. The more thoughts, emotions, and credibility are invested in the tulpa, the more real and alive they become. It's important to remember that once they've begun to exist on their own, without those who created them controlling when they appear and disappear, they're no longer imaginary, and no longer all that easy to control or get rid of.

The Yeti, or Abominable Snowman, of the Himalayas is a brilliant example of a tulpa, created by rumor and legend and then given life by increasingly widespread fear of it and belief in its existence. The native Sherpas of the high Himalayas continue to lend strength to the Yeti tulpa by firmly believing that it lives among them and that it can make itself appear and disappear at will, exactly like Alexandra David-Neel's little monk, who, once he became an actual physical being, began to decide for himself when and if he wanted to be seen.

I believe there are several other tulpas in this world, including the occasional actual sightings of demons or the devil in physical form. Take a lesson from Alexandra David-Neel: Project enough constant, obsessive fear, negativity, and evil from the core of your mind and you just might find yourself—or, much worse, as in the letter from Eva, your innocent child—being terrorized by a tulpa of your own creation, with no one but yourself to thank.

Adults are every bit as likely as children to find themselves confronted with imprints and tulpas. And there's no doubt about it, tulpas are relatively rare, but when even a handful of children have been frightened by one, as Eva's child was, they're more than worth discussing.

For you and for your children, the two greatest defenses against imprints and tulpas are the Tools of Protection you'll find in Chapter Ten of this book, and, as always, educating yourself about these and all other phenomena you and your psychic children might encounter. It bears repeating that knowledge is power. Take it from a woman who'd never heard of imprints when my son Paul was plagued by one as a child, and when I myself was scared senseless by one when I was forty years old. Only by researching them after the fact and learning what they are and what causes them was I able to become sensitive to them without being afraid of them. Please do the same for yourself and share what you learn with your child. If they understand nothing more than the basics, and that imprints can't hurt them, you will have done them an enormous favor.

And as you're educating yourself and your child about tulpas, please remember that tulpas are the physical embodiment of the saying "We create what we fear." The best protection against them is to make your home a haven safe from dark, compulsive fear, negativity, and evil. Teaching your child the important habit of projecting and surrounding themselves with nothing but the most positive, God-centered thoughts will not only help guard against tulpas; it will also lay the groundwork for the most positive, God-centered lives you can wish for them.

Familiar Smells

There's no one I cherished more on this earth than my daddy, and no one I missed more when he went Home. Never think that just because I'm psychic and can communicate with spirits from the Other Side, I have an easier time than anyone else with losing the physical presence of a loved one. I know that Daddy's living a happy, healthy, busy life at Home, and there's some comfort in that, of course. I also know, as a spiritual truth, that he comes to visit. It's not the same as having him right here beside me. Not even close. But it helps.

It's been several years since I've had glimpses of his spirit and heard his voice. But he's found a way, common in the spirit world, of letting me know he's around: I'll walk past his favorite chair in the family room, or I'll be in my car, or I'll be in the kitchen where he and I would so often just hang out and talk, and suddenly I'll get a fleeting but unmistakable whiff of a fragrance that could only come from him and no one else: his beloved cherry blend pipe tobacco. No one else in the house smokes. No one ever smokes in my car. And even if they did, my father is the only person I've ever known who smoked a pipe with no other tobacco, ever, but cherry blend. It doesn't happen often, but every time it does it's comforting and makes me smile, and I always say, right out loud, "Hi, Daddy. I love you too."

So it's no surprise at all that children, who are natural magnets for the spirit world anyway, are magnets for those whiffs of some definitive fragrance spirits often send. It's worth another reminder that spirits are always eager to have us notice them, and even the most subtle fragrances are hard for us to miss.

Paige wrote, "My grandmother used to make her own sachets to put in lingerie and linen drawers. She'd take fresh oranges and cover every inch of them with fresh cloves, and it was the coziest aroma that always made everywhere she put them smell like home to me. She passed away when I was eleven, and I hadn't really thought about those sachets ever since. But one day I heard my two-year-old daughter, Dina, playing and chatting away in her playpen, having a high old time talking to someone I couldn't hear or see. I asked her who she was talking to and she just grinned at me from ear to ear. So I walked over to her playpen to pick her up, and for the first time since I was a little girl, as I reached for her, I caught the strongest smell of oranges and cloves, just like my grandma's homemade sachets. It just lasted a few seconds, but there was no other smell like that in the world, and no one will ever convince me that my grandmother wasn't there checking up on her beautiful little great-granddaughter."

And Adrienne shared a lovely story about her three-year-old son, Adam. "The only thing my late, great dad would eat for breakfast, every morning, seven days a week, was cinnamon toast. He loved cinnamon toast, and waking up to that smell every day is a memory that makes me smile even all these twelve years since he died. We used to joke that one of the things he loved most about me was that I didn't like cinnamon toast, so he never had to share his with me. One day last week I was rushing around getting ready for work and asked Adam to go to the kitchen and get his cereal out of the cupboard for me, his way of 'helping me make his breakfast.' I was following behind a couple of minutes later, and I was a few feet from the kitchen door when I heard Adam say, 'That smells good!' I stepped into the kitchen, where he seemed to be alone, and started to ask him what smelled good, but it turned out I didn't need to. The smell of warm bread, sugar, and cinnamon—freshly made cinnamon toast—was almost overpowering. It was gone seconds later, but there's not a doubt that my son and I both smelled it, and he was standing in the middle of the room, holding his box of cereal, turned away from me and smiling up into the air as if he was looking at a tall person right in front of him. I know he was, too. He was looking at my handsome 6'3" father, who brought the aroma of his silly, favorite cinnamon toast as a gift to say hi to us from the Other Side. Not only did I have a warm sense of peace all day that day, but that night I took the time to sit down with my son and tell him all about his grandpa, since I have a feeling the two of them will be spending a lot of time together if they haven't been already."

I promise you, you'll do yourself and the children in your life an enormous service if you arm yourself with all the reliable, well-researched knowledge you can find on the various phenomena our innately psychic children might encounter and attract, from sights and sounds to coins to electrical turbulence to fragrances to the confused but ultimately harmless chaos of ghosts. Equipped with that knowledge, analyze the inevitable, seemingly unexplainable events that come along calmly, logically, and methodically. You'll be amazed at how much sense they really make, how absent of evil they really are, and how much love, comfort, and protection God has provided for His children during our brief time away from the spirit world where our eternity lies.

CHAPTER FOUR

The Past Lives of Children

If there's anything that will reassure us of our spirits' survival of death, it's the connection between children and their past lives. Their recall of having been here before is no more remarkable than our recall of what we did last week or last year, and we can learn volumes about them, and about our own eternity, if we simply listen with an open mind and stop dismissing the information they offer as either nonsense or the products of their overactive imaginations. Please don't miss the magic of the children around you, and the timeless wisdom they've brought with them, just because they're small and their vocabularies are limited. You'll be short-changing them and short-changing yourself in the process.

"When my son Steven was about two years old he would tell me that his other mommy and daddy were waking him up and playing with him during the night," Carol wrote. "And sure enough, there would be toys around on the floor in the morning that I had put away myself when I tucked him in the night before. It upset me when he talked about them, and no matter how much I explained that my husband and I were his only mommy and daddy, he insisted he had two mommies and two daddies, but the other ones just came when he was asleep. What's going on, and why is he making up another set of parents? I'd think he was just dreaming if those toys weren't all over the room."

This is a perfect example of how helpful a little education and open-mindedness would be to open up some wonderful conversations. This two-year-old was simply receiving nightly visits from the spirits of his parents in a past life, whom he loves and misses and who are undoubtedly easing his transition into this lifetime by letting him know that they're still with him. Rather than getting upset, which only teaches children to keep things to themselves, why not say, with genuine interest, "Tell me about your other mommy and daddy. Who are they? What are they like? I'd love to hear about them." Imagine how much you could learn about this new but ageless soul you've welcomed into your life by asking about his previous parents and everything else he chooses to tell you about who he was before this, especially while his memories are still so fresh and actual visits from back then are taking place.

Far more encouraging is the way Nina handled an experience with her son Billy when he was not quite four years old. "Billy was taking a bath and having a very happy conversation with someone I couldn't see. Finally I asked him who he was talking to and he said, 'My mom. Not you mom, but the mom I had before I died and God gave me you as a mom. Her name is Rachel.' I told him to tell her hello and left it at that. A few months later he was with me when I got some cash at the ATM machine, and he caught a glimpse of one of the bills and asked to see it. I handed him the twenty-dollar bill, which he stared at in amazement and then said, 'That was my dad, before the dad I have now. What's his name?' I told him it was Andrew Jackson and didn't give it any more thought. But from time to time after that he would mention something about his brother (he's an only child in this life), or comment about how mean his other dad was to 'dark-skinned people.' Somewhere along the way I got curious enough to refresh my memory about Andrew Jackson. As you probably know, he had two sons, by his wife Rachel."

What a waste if Nina had become upset and cut Billy off, instead of remaining calm and interested and discovering that she has an eyewitness to the life and times of Andrew Jackson right there in her own family.

Unless, of course, you'd prefer to believe that three-year-old Billy spent his spare time secretly watching Andrew Jackson documentaries and playing with children who happen to be Andrew Jackson buffs. But frankly, I feel safe in saying that my explanation makes more sense. Again, please don't accept or dismiss what I'm telling you about children's past lives at face value; just take the time to think. By definition, it's impossible for children to know things they couldn't possibly know from this lifetime. So where else but other lifetimes could the information have come from?

Deborah tells the story of her six-year-old son, Alex, who was mesmerized by trains from the time he was a toddler. One day as she drove him to school they stopped at a railroad crossing for a passing train. As the train roared past, Alex, without ever taking his eyes off of it, announced, "When I lived with my family in California they built a railroad to where we lived and my whole family got in the train and we went to New York." Deborah admitted that she might have written that story off to Alex's admittedly vivid imagination—although it was a stretch—but the rest of his story left her speechless: "We talked in a Spanish voice in California, but in New

York the people didn't like it if we talked in a Spanish voice." When she finally collected herself enough to come up with a response, she asked, "Alex, where was I when you were with your other family?" Without a moment's hesitation he answered, "Oh, Mom, that was while you were still with God."

Deborah, by the way, who lives in the Southwest, made it clear that her son has never been to either California or New York, and his only exposure to a Spanish voice was with some of his little schoolmates. And to this day she wonders about something she invites you all to learn from: "Why didn't I ask him years earlier where his interest in trains came from? Who knows how much of that past life he forgot by the time he was six?"

Sonjia, age two, frequently reminisced about when she was sixteen years old, living in her brother's house, and she and her baby were killed by a car. And according to Sonjia's mother, Crystal, Sonjia never talked about her baby without crying. There wasn't the slightest doubt among anyone in the family that this two-year-old child was genuinely remembering and grieving for a baby she quite obviously couldn't have given birth to in this life.

Carlo's son Clemente was five years old when he announced at a family pool party that he'd drowned before when he was two years old in the river behind his uncle's house in France. Carlo asked why he wasn't afraid of water if he'd drowned before, and Clemente replied, "Because it was okay, I went to be with God."

I have literally hundreds and hundreds of similar stories in my files and among the e-mails and letters that arrive in my office every day. And honestly, I can't imagine any child, no matter how bright or how precocious, making up stories this elaborate, this detailed, and, in some cases, so emotional. Instead, isn't it thrilling to know that these stories aren't made up at all, that they're real memories, from precious little messengers from Home who, in the end, are telling us nothing more and nothing less than that they, and we, really do survive death?

Past Lives on the Other Side

I'm not about to give up using the term *past lives,* since it's so familiar to all of us. But in a way it really is inaccurate. Rather than experiencing a series of past lives, each of us is living only one eternal life, alternating with varying frequency between incarnations on earth and our real lives on the Other Side as our spirits continue to learn and advance.

For a simple analogy, think all the way back to kindergarten and then remember each grade you progressed through as you made your way through school. Each grade was designed to teach specific lessons, depending on the appropriate level of advancement for that grade, each one building on the lessons taught in the previous grade. And because every grade was distinct from every other grade in many ways as you look back on them—different subjects, different friends, different interests, an often hilariously different variety of looks and clothing and hairstyles and maturity levels—you could reasonably think of each and every grade you went through as its own brief, essential past life. But the truth, of course, is that they're all part of the same lifetime, just as every one of your past lives is part of the same eternal lifetime of the soul.

Between one school grade and the next is the bliss of summer vacation, just as between one incarnation on earth and the next is the incomparable sacred bliss of life on the Other Side. And our ability to remember our summer vacations as clearly as we remember our school days is essentially no different than a child's ability to remember their lives at Home every bit as clearly as they remember their past lives here on earth when they're newly arrived and their memories are still fresh. If you find yourself tempted to write off their memories of life on the Other Side as meaningless childhood fantasies, please, before you do, think again when some of those memories turn out to be accurate.

Anita, who's very close to her three-year-old granddaughter, Glenna, commented to Glenna one day, "Your mommy was a little girl once upon a time just like you." Glenna replied, "I know. I saw my mommy at the hospital when she was born. My grandpa was there too." As Anita explained, "My husband, Glenna's grandpa, passed away ten years before Glenna was born, so obviously she never met him, and she definitely had no way of knowing that my husband never left my side while I was in the hospital giving birth to Glenna's mother."

And sometimes, if you listen closely, you'll even hear a child validate that they remember making choices about their upcoming trips to earth before they came here. Katina shared this conversation with her daughter Grace, whom Katina adopted when Grace was only a week old: "One day when Grace was three, I was exasperated with her and said, 'How did I ever get a little girl like you?' I was shocked when she replied, 'I picked you out.' I asked what she meant by that, and she told me, 'God lets us do that.' And she left it at that, with no further explanation."

Past Lives Within the Family

As you read in Chapter Two, my Grandma Ada came back into my life in the form of my granddaughter Angelia, and Angelia grew up with clear, accurate memories of being my grandmother. It's not all that unusual for kindred spirits to retain family relationships on their coordinated visits to earth, so please don't be surprised if you find yourself on the receiving end of a statement similar to one that Mark reported from his four-year-old daughter, Marilyn, when he presented her with a family heirloom teddy bear: "This is like the one I gave you when I was your mommy, remember, Daddy?" Unfortunately, Mark was too shocked to come up with a reply, but I can't encourage him, and you, enough to pursue those conversations and, above all, start with the assumption that they're absolutely true. I don't care if you say, "What was I like when I was a little boy back then?" or, "What else do you remember about being my mommy?" Just open the dialogue, keep it open, and follow the child's lead. You'll learn volumes about your child, not to mention the possibility, as in Mark's case, of learning volumes about yourself as well. Skeptical as you might be, wouldn't you love to hear your child tell you what you were like as a child in a past life?

Admittedly, keeping that dialogue open isn't always easy. Children don't always feel like talking on command. But then, neither do we adults, let's face it, so how critical can we be when they clam up on us?

Judy wrote about her daughter Cara, who was five years old when she asked her mother, "Do you remember when I used to rock you to sleep when I was a baby?" Judy was caught off guard, but "more than that, I was intrigued, and I started asking questions about who she was to me when she rocked me to sleep, when and where this happened, everything I could think of. Instead of answering me, she just shrugged and went to her room."

Kate's three-year-old grandson, Kevin, casually turned to her one night when she was tucking him in and matter-of-factly informed her, "I died in the car with you." Kate naturally asked him to explain, but Kevin had nothing more to say on the subject and went to sleep without another word.

Craig's four-year-old daughter, Stacie, was playing in the hallway outside his office one day and kept calling out the word, "Daddy . . . ?" Craig responded, "What?" several times, with no reply at all from Stacie. "I finally got impatient, walked to the doorway, and told her to please either tell me what she wanted or stop calling for me. She said, 'Not you, Daddy. My other daddy and mommy that died in the bomb.' I tried to question her but couldn't get any more information out of her."

Lily was four days old when she was adopted by Patricia and Luke, so they were caught completely off guard when, shortly before she turned three, Lily casually told them about life with her other family. "She said she went horseback riding by the big water with her big brother, and one time she fell off her horse and her brother made her get right back on or she would be afraid to ride her horse again. Then she went right on playing and wouldn't answer a single question we asked her about this story she'd just told us. That 'other family' sure squeezed in a lot of activity during the four days Lily was with them, though, don't you think?"

Jill's five-year-old son, Ricky, announced in the middle of breakfast one morning that "I was on this earth for twenty-three years before I came here this time. I was your mommy, and now you're my mommy. Isn't that funny?" Jill gently encouraged him to elaborate, but his cereal was suddenly more interesting to him than his announcement, and nothing more was said about it.

"When my son Robert was three years old he drew an elaborate picture that I couldn't make any sense of," Patsy wrote. "I asked him to tell me about it. He started pointing to different parts, explaining that this part is how we die, and this part is how we come back again, and this is how we were together before in another life, and this part is how when we go to heaven we have fun, and this part is when we become a baby again. He treated it like it was the most ordinary thing to draw, and then he ran off to his room with the picture. When his father got home from work I asked him to get his picture and tell Daddy about it, but he didn't want to. I retrieved the picture myself and pointed to different parts of it asking, 'What's this, Robert?' All he would do was shrug and say he didn't know, and then he took the picture back to his room and tore it up. I swear on a stack of bibles he said what he said that day, and knew what he was talking about without a doubt in his mind, but my husband is convinced I've just gone into some kind of post-partum insanity."

Joan's two-and-a-half-year-old son, Will, was sitting on her lap one night while the family watched television together, and he suddenly burst into tears. Joan asked him what was wrong. He answered, "I miss my mom and dad." Joan assured him that she was right there with him, and his dad was on the sofa beside them, but he shook his head and kept crying, "No, my *real* mom and dad." "It startled me, but I didn't let him see that and just asked him to tell me about them. He explained that his 'real mom' died of cancer and his 'real dad' died in a car accident. I asked when it happened and what their names were, but he didn't want to discuss it any further."

There's no doubt about it, no matter how beautifully you handle it, there really is no guaranteed way to get a child to open up about their past-life memories beyond what they're ready to share, when and if they volunteer the information. There are questions you can ask them, like "Who were you before this?" and "Have you had other mommies and daddies before us?" and "Have you and I ever known each other before now?" They may or may not give you answers at the time you ask. But at least they'll know you're interested and available for those conversations, and that in itself is a wonderful gift to offer children as they struggle to acclimate themselves to this strange, imperfect place called earth.

Another gift, to children and to yourself, is one I can't encourage you enough to undertake: I want you to keep a journal of every bit of information your child gives you about their past lives, both here and on the Other Side, even if you're suffering under the illusion that they're just making it up. The sad fact is, it's very likely that by the time your child reaches their teens, they won't remember the vast wealth of knowledge and memories they brought with them from Home. And it's perfect logic that they, and we, do tend to forget. We're here to concentrate on this lifetime, to accomplish the goals that compelled us to come here again in the first place as we outlined in the charts we so meticulously wrote to guarantee the success of those goals. We're not meant to be preoccupied with our past lives, or the bliss of our lives on the Other Side. We have our hands full with the work we're here to do this time around. But writing down a child's specific awareness of their immortality will reassure them—and you—in later years, when their conscious minds have forgotten, that their eternal spirit minds are alive, well, and holding all that beautiful God-given wisdom for safekeeping.

Also in that journal I want you to take notes on any special interests your child seems to have been born with, particularly in things they couldn't possibly have been exposed to during their brief time

on earth this time around. Of course, first you have to pause to ac-
knowledge that those special interests aren't just haphazard flukes;
they're very real spotlights on your child's past lives, here, at Home
or both. I can't tell you how often I hear, professionally and socially,
a perfectly intelligent adult say something like, "My little girl has
been obsessed with horses from the minute she first laid eyes on
one," or, "All my child has to do is glance at a picture of a train, or
see one on TV, and he goes crazy. He's never even been near a train
in real life, so I don't know what that's about." And I always say to
them what I'll say to you: Don't just sit there, ask them. Don't make
a big deal out of it to your child, or put it in the form of a challenge,
like "Why are you so interested in that?" which might make them
defensive. Instead, try a simple "Have you ever had a horse of your
own?" or, "Have you ridden on a train before?" Chances are you'll get
an answer that will give you at least a glimpse into your child's history before the two of you met.

Dominique tells the story of an incident with her son Jay when
he hadn't yet turned three years old. "My husband and I love all
kinds of music, and it's almost always playing in the family room of
our house. My child Jay didn't seem interested in it or even seem to
notice it until one night when we were watching a wonderful or-
chestral concert on television. There was a passage that featured
nothing but the violins. Jay's head suddenly whipped around to the
TV, his eyes got huge, and he toddled over to it as fast as he could,
touched the screen with both hands, and started saying, 'Mama!
Mama!' over and over again. It was the strangest thing I've ever seen.
We've been watching him more closely since that night, and there's
no doubt about it, he reacts immediately and very happily to the
specific sound of violin music. What's this about? Do we have a
budding violin virtuoso on our hands?"

Not exactly, Dominique. You have a child whose mother in his previous life in the late 1800s was a violin virtuoso with the London Symphony Orchestra. He was an only child whose mother adored him and shared her love of classical music, and specifically the violin, with him rather than send him off with his nanny to keep him out of the way. It speaks volumes about his joy in that life that he charted two parents in this life who love music as well, so don't be surprised if he chooses a profession in the music field this time around.

Three-year-old Amber's father, Joe, noticed that from the time Amber was old enough to walk she would rush to the window and excitedly point to the sky every time she heard a plane fly overhead. Out of curiosity he bought a couple of picture books of airplanes and simply left them where she could reach them, mixed in with picture books on other subjects. She quickly picked out the airplane books and was mesmerized by the photographs. She would hold up one after the other to show to her parents, saying, "Pane! Pane!" (the closest she could come to "plane" at the time), and Joe stressed in his letter that Amber had never been on or even near an airplane in this lifetime. "One morning while I was having breakfast she came running into the kitchen with one of her books opened to a picture of a World War II bomber, climbed into my lap with it, and said, 'I fly this.' I couldn't believe my ears, but my wife heard her too. We tried asking her to tell us more about it; we just couldn't compete with her fascination with that section of the book. Maybe we're crazy, but we're convinced that our little girl was once a fighter pilot in the Second World War. We've booked a flight to go visit my parents next month, and we can't wait to see her reaction to being on a 'pane' for the first time."

No, you're not crazy, Joe. Your little girl was a decorated Air

Force pilot in World War II, a male whose name was Cliff or Clifton, and he died of heart failure completely unrelated to his lifelong love of flying.

There really is nothing haphazard about those things that spark a child's most intent interests seemingly out of nowhere. It's reliable to assume that those interests are reflections of their past lives, or of their full, busy lives on the Other Side.

Similarly, there's nothing haphazard about some of the fears and physical and mental challenges a child is born with. To understand those, you have to understand a very real and fascinating concept called cell memory.

Children and Cell Memory

I've written extensively on the subject of cell memory, including in my book *Past Lives, Future Healing*. Knowing what cell memory is, how it affects all of us, and how to address it in children can make a profound improvement in the rest of their lives.

Cell memory is the total body of knowledge our spirit minds have gathered during all our past lives on earth, infused into every cell of our bodies and then reacted to by those cells the moment our spirit enters the fetus shortly before we're born. It's the key to resolving countless health problems, phobias, night terrors, and any number of psychological obstacles a child might need to overcome.

A step-by-step explanation of cell memory goes like this:

✳ We know that our bodies are made up of billions of interacting cells.

✳   We know that each of those cells is a living, feeling organism that receives and follows orders in a very literal way from whatever information is transmitted to it by the subconscious mind. For example, if we're told under hypnosis, when the subconscious mind is more in charge than the conscious mind, that the hypnotist's finger is actually a lighted match and that finger touches our arm, the cells of our arm will form a blister, just as they're programmed to do when they come in contact with a flame.

✳   It's in the subconscious that our spirit minds exist, remembering every moment we've experienced, in this life and every other life we've lived since we were created.

✳   The instant our spirit minds enter our physical bodies for a new incarnation, they're flooded with the familiarity of being in a body, and all those memories and sensations from past incarnations come rushing back. If you've ever revisited a place that holds powerful memories for you and found yourself having physical and emotional reactions to being there again, you've had a glimpse of what our spirits experience when they find themselves in a body again.

✳   Our subconscious minds, on receiving all this new information, promptly infuse it into the billions of cells that make up our bodies, and those cells dutifully respond to that information as their reality. And they continue to react physiologically to all the memories from past lives that our spirit minds infuse them with, whether our conscious minds are aware of those memories or not.

✳ And so, by accessing those cell memories and understanding that they're part of lives and deaths we've already moved on from, we can rid ourselves of long-buried illness, phobias, pain, and trauma and give ourselves a clean slate to work with in this new incarnation.

I've worked with literally thousands of clients whose lives have been completely transformed thanks to the unearthing of cell memories that are holding them back. I can't stress enough that the pursuit of cell-memory answers should never take the place of working with licensed, reputable medical and psychiatric professionals to get to the root of a problem. I can be an effective supplement to those professionals, but I'm not a replacement for them. And it delights me to know that more and more of them are accepting the possibility (read "fact") that not every physical, physiological, emotional, or mental malady can be traced to a source in this current lifetime.

In addition to being a psychic, I'm also a certified master hypnotist, and I've had great success using both skills to get to the core of children's cell memories from past lives that are causing current, very real disturbances. And children are wonderful hypnosis subjects, take it from someone who's hypnotized thousands of them. Between their innate willingness to trust and their wide-open connections to their spirit minds, they're a joy to work with.

In fact, a great demonstration of the power of cell memory is a six-year-old boy named Greg, whose parents, at their wits' end, brought him to me for a hypnosis session in the hope of relieving his severe asthma and his hyperactivity. They'd already been to countless doctors, and Greg was on medication for both conditions. Here's a surprise: The medication didn't seem to be helping. (When problems are rooted in cell memories, it's very rare for medication to make a difference.)

Greg was an only child, a smart, funny little boy who'd already made casual passing comments to his parents that made it clear he had conscious memories of past lives. He'd told his mother that he remembered when he was *her* mother, and he'd announced one day at a family party that "I know all about boats," even though he'd never been anywhere near one in this life. So I knew that helping him remember more details about those previous lives through hypnosis would be a breeze.

There were two past lives that seemed to be the most memorable to Greg. In one of them he was happily married to a woman named Anna. They had eleven children and lived on a farm with lots of animals. He was called away to fight in the war as a naval officer and was killed when his ship was attacked and a piece of shrapnel pierced his throat. In the second life Greg vividly remembered he was a woman, the widowed mother of nine children (one of whom was "my mommy now," he was amused to report) whose household and life in general seemed like perpetual chaos. In that life he died of pneumonia at the age of thirty-eight.

Two lifetimes that ended abruptly due to breathing-related catastrophes, and in this lifetime the child has asthma that's not responding to medication. Two lifetimes in which the households were constantly chaotic with lots of noisy, active children, and in this lifetime Greg is a hyperactive only child, again, not responding to medication. He listened raptly, still under hypnosis, as I assured him that he was only having these problems because the cells of his body thought they were still living those previous lives. He could release those problems now, because they'd been resolved when those lives ended, and go on with his new life healthy, happy, and peaceful.

Six months after my regressive hypnosis session with Greg, his parents reported that his asthma attacks had become virtually nonexistent and that his hyperactivity had calmed to the point that his teacher was sure he'd changed to a more effective medication, when in fact he was no longer taking any medication at all. I still remember the call from Greg's pediatrician, who'd first prescribed and then weaned Greg off of Ritalin when the dramatic improvement in his behavior became apparent. "I don't know what you did," he told me, "but it sure worked."

And after all, that's the whole point: not whether I'm right or wrong, but whether something works, and works risk-free. Again, you'll never hear me advocate replacing doctors' orders with cell-memory work, but you will hear me advocate helping to eliminate any harmful cell memories your children may have brought with them from other lives they've lived, right along with any recommendations their doctors have to offer. There's no either/or choice to make between my advice and your doctors'. Be as skeptical as you like; just be open-minded enough to try it, if only to prove that I don't know what I'm talking about. Then let the positive results you see in your children speak for themselves.

You don't need access to a regressive hypnotherapist, or even to a reputable psychic who's able to do accurate past life readings, to help flush out a child's negative cell memories. There's invariably simple logic in the connection between then and now, particularly in children whose past lives still seem so recent to them. The minute you stop thinking of it as a haphazard array of fears, physical and mental challenges, and behavior problems and apply that logic instead, you can make significant headway in getting to the root of and then relieving the problem.

An urgent call from a friend of a friend sent me to the home of a woman named Arlene, who needed help with her two-year-old son, Ben. He was a normal, happy little boy, with one exception: at the sight of his mother preparing to step into the shower, Ben would fly into an out-of-control panic, screaming, "No, Mama, no!" crying so hard he could barely breathe and trying desperately to pull her out of the bathroom. I saw his hysteria with my own eyes when his mother, to demonstrate, pretended to be getting ready for a shower. It was heartbreaking and horribly traumatic for both of them, and as we calmed him down I explained what I psychically knew was going on: In his previous life, this child and his family had been imprisoned in the unspeakably inhuman concentration camp at Dachau, and he'd witnessed his mother being gassed to death in the showers there. The seemingly innocent sight of his mother in this life heading toward a harmless present-tense shower in the safety of their own home triggered that hideous cell memory, to the point where Ben's whole being believed his mother wouldn't survive that shower.

When he was finally calm again, exhausted but reassured that Arlene was alive and well, she and I tucked him into bed and I taught her how to help him while he slept, using a very simple technique you'll find later in this chapter. She tried this technique every night from then on, and in less than a month Ben gave no thought whatsoever to the sight of his mother stepping into a shower.

Please don't think for a moment that I'm suggesting Arlene should have been able to figure out that her two-year-old son was equating mother-and-shower with the past-life horror of Dachau. Being psychic comes in handy for filling in details like that. But taking the very real impact of cell memory into account, whether you know the details or not, can help explain all sorts of seemingly inexplicable childhood behavior, especially when you apply basic, general logic like, "My child is repeatedly upset by this specific circumstance, so some form of this specific circumstance is clearly an unresolved cell memory from a past life."

To give just a few examples from my files:

* A child with extreme claustrophobia who, through hypnosis, remembered a past life in which he died in a mining collapse.
* A child with a fear of heights who remembered dying as the result of a fall from a cliff in Hawaii, where he lay with a broken back waiting for a rescue crew that didn't find him in time.
* A child who would only consume food and liquids that had been prepared and served while she watched—the result of a past-life poisoning by a greedy son who wanted to hurry along his inheritance.
* A child utterly terrified by thunderstorms who, in his most recent past life, died while caught at sea on a small fishing boat during a hurricane.

A variation on these logical manifestations of a child's cell memory is described in a letter from Peggy, who was understandably deeply concerned about her son Grant. "Shortly before Grant was born we had the good fortune to inherit a wonderful country home with a long driveway that includes a wooden bridge over a creek that runs the length of our property. For the first four years of his life he loved every square inch of this place as we do. But several months ago, shortly before his fifth birthday, we were coming home from a trip into town and when we got to the bridge, Grant started scream- ing bloody murder and was pounding on the car door wanting us to stop and let him out. We couldn't imagine what had gotten into him and we kept driving, but it took forever to get him to calm down, and he couldn't explain what was wrong. He just kept saying he didn't want to go on that bridge anymore. If it had only happened one time it would have been scary enough, but he's been frightened of the bridge ever since, even when we try to walk him across it to remind him how safe it is. And it's not like we can avoid the bridge, since it's part of the only route from our house to the main road. What's going on with Grant, and how can we help him get over this? We're at our wits' end!"

What's going on with Grant is actually a cell-memory experience that's very common among both children and adults. In his specific case, he died in a past life when the school bus he was riding in swerved out of control on a bridge to avoid an oncoming truck, broke through the railings, and plunged into the river below. And most significantly, he was five years old when he died in that life. The trauma of that cell memory is causing his spirit mind to say, "I'm in a body again, and when I was in a body before I died going off a bridge at the age of five. There's a bridge, and I'm about to turn five, so I must be in grave danger."

Again, the examples of these age-related cell memories from my files go on and on:

* A nine-year-old who, seemingly out of nowhere, was terrified when his father lit the backyard barbecue grill was killed in a previous life in a house fire at the age of nine.
* A six-year-old who went from loving his swimming lessons to hiding from his mother in an effort to escape them because of a drowning death at age six in a past life.
* A three-year-old who'd always had a perfectly normal appetite became insatiable, screaming for food at all hours of

the day and night, thanks to a past life death at the age of three due to malnutrition.

✳ An eight-year-old girl who, due to her death in a previous incarnation at eight years old from a fall down the stairs that broke her neck, suddenly refused to venture upstairs in her family's two-story house.

So if a child you know—or an adult, for that matter—develops an unexpected fear that has no apparent cause in this lifetime, it's probable, I promise you, that its roots can be found in an age-specific cell memory from another life. They're not random phobias, any more than the supposedly inexplicable special interests a child is born with are random. They're all part of the continuum of our eternal spirits, perfectly logical results of the fact that none of us, even as newborns, arrive here without a rich, timeless past.

Please don't let me create the impression that all cell memories are negative or harmful. It's cell memory that contributes to the genius of child prodigies. It's cell memory that inspires some children to talk while they sleep in a foreign language they've never been exposed to or understood a word of when they're awake. It's cell memory that, on occasion, causes a child to completely heal from an illness doctors have declared incurable, thanks to a previous life in which the child remembers almost dying and then fully recovering from a similar illness or at the same age. And sometimes it's cell memory that solves murders, as happened in a wonderful story a surgeon friend shared with me:

Molly was ten years old when she received a heart transplant from a seventeen-year-old stabbing victim named David, whose murder was unsolved, with very few clues and no likely suspects.

Months after the transplant, Molly began having nightmares about a dark figure in a ski mask stalking her, chasing her, lying in wait for her, always with a knife in his hand. Through hypnosis, Molly was eventually able to remove the dark figure's ski mask and identify a young man named Martin. Martin wasn't a name or a face from Molly's life. In fact, she'd never heard of him. Instead, he was an acquaintance of David's who mistakenly believed David had stolen money from his school locker. The police were shown a videotape of the hypnosis session in which Molly described Martin in detail and gave his first name, and he was brought in for questioning. Martin finally confessed to the murder, all thanks to David's cell memory, infused throughout the body of a little girl who had the courage to share information that only David could possibly have known.

The Point of Entry

If you sense that a child is troubled by cell memories from past lives that they're unable to remember clearly or are having trouble verbalizing, it might be helpful to you and the child to know about a concept called the "point of entry."

A point of entry is simply the core event or core lifetime that created the cell memory to begin with. It was my Spirit Guide Francine who introduced the point of entry concept to me. I'd been doing regressive hypnosis therapy for several months, and I'd had countless sessions in which clients were so enchanted with the novelty of revisiting their past lives that it took them forever to get to the one that was interfering with their current lives. It wasn't boring, but it was inefficient as far as specific problem solving was concerned. When Francine suggested that, during hypnosis, I direct my clients to go to their point of entry, I couldn't have been more skeptical. As I said to her, "*I don't know what 'point of entry' means. How can I expect my clients to know what it means?*" But she promised me two things that convinced me to try it. One was that it's a term the spirit mind understands, whether the conscious mind gets it or not. The other was that the spirit mind will leap at every opportunity to be cleansed and healed.

I took Francine's advice with my regressive hypnosis clients, telling them to go to their point of entry if and when they started wandering aimlessly from one previous life to another, and I was shocked at their immediate response. Not one client ever asked what point of entry meant. Instead, every one of them jumped directly to the lifetime, and the experience in that lifetime, where the cell memory they were struggling with began.

The vast majority of adults need the help of hypnosis, meditation, or sleep to make a clear connection to their spirit minds. Children, on the other hand, have ready access to them. I don't guarantee success with asking a wide-awake child whose past lives seem to be debilitating them in this life if they know what their point of entry was. But there's not a shred of harm in trying, and there will be an occasional child who can answer that question and who will be liberated by it.

Healing a Child's Cell Memories

I can guarantee success, though, with a simple exercise that will benefit every child in your life. It doesn't matter how many days or years old the child is. It doesn't matter whether or not they're showing signs of being plagued by cell memories, let alone what the details and points of entry those cell memories might involve. It doesn't even matter if you're only giving it a try to prove that I don't have the first clue what I'm talking about. It only matters that you try it. Be consistent about it, and keep it up until you see results. It might take a week, it might take a month. But it's an investment of less than five minutes of your time that can give your child greater peace, confidence, and potential success throughout their lifetime.

Every night while the child is sound asleep, I want you to sit or kneel beside them quietly enough not to disturb them. In your mind, I want you to completely surround them from head to toe with the most brilliantly glowing white light you can possibly imagine, creating a halo of God's love around every inch of their body.

Keeping your voice in a clear whisper that won't wake the child, I want you to offer them cleansing and healing by speaking to the wise, ancient spirit mind that's housed in that little body and on constant vigil for an acknowledgment that it even exists. Assuringly repeat this prayer, or your own version of it:

> Precious child, may all the joy, wisdom, and love from your past lives be your constant companions as you make your way through this life. But with God's help, let go of all the pain, fear, illness, and negativity from those lives so that they can be released from you and resolved forever in this pure, healing, sacred white light of the Holy Spirit that surrounds you now and always, like God's unconditional love for you.

If you find it hard to believe that something so easy will work, that's okay. I believe it enough for both of us. I've seen it make a genuine difference in children's physical and emotional health time and time and time again. And on the off chance that I'm right, what do you possibly have to lose by trying?

Birthmarks

When I was about nine years old I noticed a slightly angry-looking red mark on the inside of my Grandma Ada's upper right arm. I was upset, thinking she'd hurt herself, and I reached to touch it, but she pulled away, asking me to leave it alone because it was a little sensitive. She assured me that it was okay, nothing had happened, it was just a birthmark, a scar from a previous life when she'd been badly burned by a fireplace poker.

As a very psychic nine-year-old, I knew we've all had previous lives, and even then I didn't understand why some people seemed to doubt something so obvious. Probably because it was something I took for granted. I also wasn't all that interested in it, or in birthmarks either, for that matter. I was just relieved that Grandma Ada was okay and didn't give it another thought.

Decades later, my cherished granddaughter Angelia was born, and, as you read in Chapter Two, we were all stunned to realize that she was Grandma Ada, back from the Other Side to be with me again in the form of this breathtaking child. And suddenly that moment with my grandmother came rushing back to me when I saw, on Angelia's upper right arm, a birthmark identical to Ada's. Angelia's was on the outside of her arm rather than the inside, but exactly the same distance from her shoulder, as if my grandmother was giving me a physical sign that she was back in case I missed all the other overwhelming clues.

I'd actually begun studying birthmarks years before Angelia was born, at the passing request of a neurologist friend who was convinced that there was some significance to birthmarks, rather than their just being random flukes of pigmentation. Knowing I saw between fifteen and twenty clients a day for readings and/or the regressive hypnosis I was doing by then, he asked if I would casually poll them about their birthmarks, if they had them, and see if I could come up with any connection to congenital diseases, neurological disorders, or anything else that might occur to me.

I agreed. Unenthusiastically, I admit it. I wasn't especially interested in birthmarks (I thought), and as much respect as I had for my neurologist friend, I was sure he was overthinking this particular subject (I thought). But it wasn't a big favor for him to ask, so I promised to do what I could if it wouldn't be disruptive for my clients.

My first appointment the next morning was a past-life regression with a man who, while under hypnosis, described dying in a past life by bleeding to death from a knife wound in the back of his right leg, three or four inches below the knee.

As an afterthought, when he was fully awake and about to leave my office, I asked if by any chance he happened to have any birthmarks.

He did, and he showed it to me—a brown-red oval mark about two inches long, on the back of his right leg, three or four inches below the knee. Exactly where a knife had pierced and killed him a couple of centuries ago.

It genuinely shocked me. But one client with a coincidentally located birthmark proves nothing. So I began asking client after client after client the same question if they'd mentioned a past-life wound or violent death during regressive hypnosis. And nine out of ten times, they showed me a birthmark that corresponded to the wound they described. In fact, over all these years it's become rare to find clients who don't still have some visible trace of a previous incarnation.

It took me longer than it should have to realize what a natural, logical extension of cell memory birthmarks really are. If cell memory can make a dramatic emotional and psychological impact on our present lifetimes, why shouldn't it have the potential to make a dramatic physical impact as well?

Douglas wrote about his daughter Lola, who was born with a crescent-shaped brown birthmark behind and below her left ear. She was not quite three years old when he spontaneously pointed to it and asked her what it was. "I was planning to explain to her that it was a birthmark. But out of nowhere she said, 'Where a hammer hit me.' I couldn't imagine what brought that on, or why she knew the word *hammer,* but I told her that a hammer didn't hit her, it was called a birthmark and she had it since the day she was born. She said, 'No, Daddy, *before.*' It really threw me, she was so insistent, and what's funny is, it even looks like the head of a hammer."

Cathy's son Cody was born with a spear-shaped birthmark on his lower back. "When he was five years old he told me he was afraid of knives, to the point where he would even push them away at the dinner table, and he said it was because he was stabbed. Thanks to Sylvia's writing about past lives I understood, instead of freaking out about my five-year-old thinking he had been stabbed."

"I was told when I was a child that the small birthmark on my cheek was an Angel's kiss, and it made me happy about my birthmark," wrote Natasha. "So when my daughter Jana was three or four I wanted to do the same thing for her about the V-shaped birthmark on her wrist. We were standing beside each other one morning looking in the full-length mirror in my bedroom, and I said, 'Did you know that your birthmark is from where an Angel kissed you as you were being born?' She said, 'No, it was from a bird.' I said, 'What?' and she told me, 'It's okay, Mommy, it was when I was big. It doesn't hurt now.'"

After a few decades of nearly identical stories, and my own

lovely experience with Angelia and the birthmark that was like a miraculous subtle wink from Grandma Ada, my skepticism is long gone. I can promise you that, as I eventually reported to my neurologist friend, there's great significance to about nine birthmarks out of ten—they're delivered by cell memory as physical proof of some previous lifetime.

If you're close to a child with a birthmark, casually ask them where it came from. Then open your mind, do your spirit a favor and listen. There's a good chance they'll be able to tell you about a past life trauma that corresponds to that birthmark, which will allow you a glimpse into the history of that child's spirit and, in the process, a glimpse into your own eternal birthright.

CHAPTER FIVE

At Home in Two Places: Psychic Children and the Other Side

Children have an intimate, readily accessible relationship with the Other Side. It's the safe, idyllic, blissful Home they've just left behind to come to this strange, rough place called earth. They volunteered to make the trip, and they designed each and every aspect of it, but they arrive Homesick and, for at least a few years, more at ease with the dimension of the Other Side than with the much slower frequency we live with here.

Of course, we were all children once, and that same intimate connection to Home was as natural to us as breathing and as familiar as our loved ones are to us now. And one of the questions I'm asked most often is: If that's true, why do we seem to lose our awareness of the Other Side, or at least our memory of it? It would make it so much easier to believe in, and we'd be so much less afraid.

The answer is frustratingly logical: If we spent our lifetimes on earth with a perpetual consciousness of Home, we'd never make the commitment to being here and accomplishing the goals we set for ourselves toward the growth and advancement of our spirits. On the most simplistic level, it would be like being stuck in a classroom every day with a clear view of Disneyland in full swing right outside the window. I wouldn't get much schoolwork done, or care, would you? So against a backdrop of our God-given eternity, it makes perfect sense that our conscious awareness of the Other Side slowly fades as we adjust to a new lifetime on earth, even if it does leave us with a lifelong sense of Homesickness we can never quite put our finger on until we leave this earth again and return to the sacred embrace of God's arms.

Until then, we have the fresh memories, the clarity and the unapologetic innocence of children to make up for everything we've forgotten about that divine, perfect world and its blessed residents. And all we have to do is open our minds and hearts and listen.

Children and their Spirit Guides

In Chapter Two you read about my introduction to my Spirit Guide Francine, who announced herself in my bedroom one night when I was seven years old and scared me senseless. I want to make it clear now if I didn't make it clear then: The significance of that story isn't the fact that I was and am psychic, or that there was something unique about my having a Spirit Guide. The significance of that story is that I first met my Spirit Guide when I was a child, which makes me and that experience far more common than you might imagine.

Every one of us has a Spirit Guide, someone we chose and literally trusted with our soul on the Other Side when we made the decision to come to earth for another lifetime. To clear up a common area of confusion, they're not a loved one who passed on after we were born—by definition, they were at Home with us at the time we were writing our charts and preparing for another incarnation. So when you're wondering who your Spirit Guide is, you can immediately rule out anyone who wasn't already on the Other Side at the moment of your birth, and you shouldn't be surprised or disappointed to learn that your Spirit Guide is someone you've never heard of. It's impossible for you to have heard of them here on earth. Our relationship with our Spirit Guide always precedes this particular lifetime.

Our Spirit Guides made a holy, ironclad contract with us on the Other Side to be our constant, vigilant companions during this incarnation. They've all experienced at least one lifetime on earth themselves, so the problems, mistakes, temptations, fears, and frailties inevitable in us humans aren't as incomprehensible as they would be if they'd never been human themselves. Their sacred commitment is to gently and quietly advise, support, and guide us along our chosen path, with our charts in hand to help keep us on track toward our intended goals.

Spirit Guides won't interfere with the choices we make, or deprive us of our free will. At best, they offer possible alternatives and warnings. But our agreement with them is that we're here to grow, and to advance the journey of our souls, and they know we can't accomplish that if they constantly shield us from the lessons we need to learn.

They communicate with us adults in a variety of ways, sending messages, most often through our spirit minds but occasionally audibly, that are usually mistaken for instincts, or hunches, or problem-solving dreams, or all sorts of variations on "something told me to . . ."

Like the rest of the spirit world, though, Guides have a far more direct line to the children who just said good-bye to them on the Other Side. It's not uncommon for children to clearly hear their Spirit Guides, like I did, and to see them, which only happened to me once, fleetingly, when I was in my late teens. Their Guides will look and sound as real to them as we do, for one very good reason: They *are* real, and they're here to fulfill their sacred oath to God that the child in their care will never take a step or draw a breath without them until that child has returned Home again, safe and sound.

Children may not recognize the identity or significance of their Spirit Guide when they show up. They might perceive their Guide as nothing more than just another friend from the spirit world who's stopped by to visit and play. Pay attention to the frequency with which your child refers to visits from the same spirit. If you hear the same name mentioned over and over again as a seemingly constant companion—in other words, someone you might assume is your child's imaginary friend—that's one clue that it might be their Spirit Guide. If it's no one you recognize as a family member or other loved one who's passed on, that's another clue. If your child never refers to the visiting spirit as having any injuries or physical challenges, and never perceives the spirit to be unhappy or behaving badly or saying negative things (all of which would mean it's a confused earthbound ghost, not a spirit), that's still another clue. Last but not least, if the information your child receives from the visiting spirit is God-centered, spiritually nurturing, prophetic, and infallibly accurate, that's the most significant clue of all.

"My son Daren was three years old," Kate wrote. "We were on a shopping trip when out of the blue he 'introduced' me to his new friend Morton and asked if Morton could come home and live with us. Daren was standing there by himself but was acting as if Morton was right beside him. So I 'shook hands' with Morton and said he was welcome in our house if he promised to be a good boy and be nice to Daren. Morton has been with Daren ever since, sleeping under his bed and having long talks with him. I never need to ask what they talk about, because Daren is a chatterbox and is always excited to tell me. Morton tells him about Heaven, and about how we all live many lives, and that when we die Angels come to get us. Daren even told me that I was going to have a baby before my husband and I had a chance to tell him I was pregnant, because Morton spilled the beans."

And if the presence of the Spirit Guide frightens your child as it did me at first, don't assume the presence is evil. It turned out that mine wasn't, God knows. Take the approach my Grandma Ada took with me, tell them their Spirit Guide has come to visit and explain to them what a wonderful, helpful, special friend their Spirit Guide will be to them for the rest of their lives. Whether or not your child seems to consciously understand, their spirit mind will—just as with us adults, no matter how much noise and confusion the conscious mind has to bat its way through in the course of a day, the spirit mind *always* knows the truth when it hears it.

Philip was caring for his two-year-old grandson, Dennis, when Dennis began screaming from amid his toys on the floor where he was playing by himself. "Nander touched my head, Pawpaw! Nander touched my head!" Everything looked perfectly normal to Philip as he raced to pick up Dennis, who was pointing to his head where "Nander" had touched him. There was no mark of any kind. "Needless to say, I'd never heard of anyone named Nander before, so while I calmed Dennis down with a bowl of cereal I asked him if Nander had hurt him. He said no. I asked him if Nander was bad, and he said, 'No, he good, Pawpaw. He big like you.' Before I could find out why Dennis was scared if Nander was good, Dennis added, 'Daddy coming today.' I explained that no, his daddy wasn't picking him up until three days from then, when he was back from his trip. But Dennis said, 'No, today. Nander said.' I knew that was wrong, so I ignored it and went on to announce loudly to Nander that he was welcome around my grandson if he was good, but he wasn't welcome to scare him anymore, so maybe he should find another way of communicating with him. That seemed to make Dennis happy, and he went back to playing with his toys. You could have knocked me over with the proverbial feather when about an hour later my son Eddie, Dennis's father, came walking in, home from his trip three days early. Dennis wasn't surprised at all and just looked at me and smiled, 'See? Nander said.' Dennis was never frightened by Nander again, and until he was about ten or eleven years old he had dreams in which he and Nander played in the park and Nander told him nice things about Heaven. And I think he was six years old when I mentioned Nander and Dennis corrected me—it wasn't Nander, it was *Alexander*."

Frankly, Dennis did a lot better than I did with his first encounter with his Spirit Guide Alexander than I did when Francine introduced herself. If she had touched me in addition to speaking to me, I might have run screaming from the house and never turned back. But if you're wondering how and why I know this was Dennis's Spirit Guide, and how you can know in similar situations of your own, the answer is simply that the child was told something by "Nander" that was going to happen, which he had no possible way of knowing and which turned out to be true: that his father was coming home three days early.

And then there was Janet's daughter Danielle, whose imaginary playmate Matthew began appearing to Danielle when she was three. Matthew was "the same size as me," according to Danielle, with "yellow hair," and "he makes my toys float around." (Like the rest of the spirit world, Spirit Guides will very often move animate objects for no other reason than to get our attention.) The rest of the family indulged Danielle's imagination, leaving room for Matthew on the sofa while watching TV if Danielle insisted, tucking him in beside Danielle at night at her request, even holding his invisible hand along with Danielle's when they crossed the street. They were purely humoring her until one day when Danielle was seven and ran to her father in a panic as he left for work, urgently begging, "Don't take the bridge to work, Daddy. Matthew says don't take the bridge." "My husband always took the Bay Bridge into the city to work every morning," Janet explained, "but Danielle was so frantic that he promised her he would take the long route that day, even though it would take him a half hour out of his way. As it turned out, it was a lucky thing he always kept promises to his daughter. There was a tragic multi-car accident on the bridge that morning, with six fatalities. Even though the accident happened before my husband would have arrived, the bridge and the highway leading to it were gridlocked for hours, with traffic at a dead standstill, and my husband would have missed an important meeting. Matthew never passed along anything else that made that big an impression, but we'll always remember and thank him for that one."

Janet's story illustrates an excellent point about Spirit Guides that I want to emphasize in case there's any confusion. As I mentioned in Chapter One, when we're at Home on the Other Side, we're all thirty years old. But visitors from the Other Side, including

Spirit Guides, can appear here on earth at any age that might help us recognize them or put us at maximum ease. "Nander," in the first story, was described by Dennis as being "big" like his grandfather, which means he probably appeared in his natural thirty-year-old spirit form, while Danielle's Spirit Guide Matthew was the same size as she was at the age of three. Just please don't rule it in or out that a visiting spirit is your child's Spirit Guide based solely on your child's description of their size or age.

One of the most fascinating and often overlooked aspects of Spirit Guides is that they talk to each other, behind our backs, so to speak, with our charts in hand. They share information that might be valuable to those of whom each other are in charge, knowledge to pass along to those of us who are receptive to messages from the spirit world—and, as we've seen again and again, that definitely includes children.

Sarah was six years old when she came downstairs in her pajamas one morning, headed straight to her father Bradley at the breakfast table, gave him a big hug and said, "Don't be sad about Dean, Daddy. He's in heaven, and he's sending you a dove." Bradley had become accustomed to odd, sometimes incomprehensible remarks from his daughter since she was old enough to talk, especially after long, seemingly one-sided talks with her invisible friend Gail. And he'd learned over the years to dismiss them as childish nonsense. As he admitted in his letter, "I was an avowed nonbeliever, an orthodox Catholic, with no patience for spirituality talk and no patience for my wife's belief that Gail was my daughter's Spirit Guide. It was all nonsense as far as I was concerned. I hated to break it to my daughter, but I didn't know anyone named Dean, and I told her so. She said, 'Yes you do. Gail told me.'

"That afternoon my mom called, and I repeated my conversation with Sarah, thinking she'd get a kick out of. Instead, she said I did know someone named Dean; he and I were childhood friends when our families lived across the street from each other, and he'd died two days earlier from heart failure. If that didn't shock me enough, when I went to the parking lot that night after work there was a dove just sitting there on the hood of my car. I know it was probably a coincidence, but it's sure given me a lot of food for thought."

Which brings up another important point about the communication between children and their Spirit Guides. If there's any word more popular than imagination among hardcore skeptics, it's the word *coincidence*. So let me clear up once and for all what coincidences really are.

When we write our charts on the Other Side before coming here for another incarnation, we include a series of little flagged events. They're not necessarily significant; we simply highlight them as progress markers along our earthly journey. When a coincidence happens in our lives, it means that we've had a fleeting conscious memory of one of those markers shortly before we charted it to occur. You suddenly think of someone you haven't thought of in a while, for example, and by coincidence they happen to call. By the real definition of coincidence, you charted that they would call when they did, and your conscious mind remembered ahead of time, just for an instant, writing that seemingly trivial event into your chart. In truth, it's a wonderful convergence of your life on the Other Side when you wrote your chart and your life here on earth when you're acting it out. It's a sign that you're on track, and it's worthy of more than a passing glance—it's worthy of celebration, confirmation that you and your chart are in perfect step.

So on one hand, yes, the story of Sarah, Gail, and Sarah's father, Bradley, is a coincidence that he wrote into his chart—in his case, a relatively inconsequential event to jump-start a fresh look at his spiritual beliefs, thanks to his daughter's knowing something she couldn't have known and even predicting a sign that she was right. From another angle, it's also a case of Bradley's Spirit Guide seeing the flagged moment in his chart and passing the information along to Sarah's Spirit Guide to make sure Bradley was paying attention.

Dorian shared another wonderful story of Spirit Guides communicating with each other—in this case, her Guide getting an alert from her seven-year-old daughter, Jona's Guide that something was very wrong. "One day last summer I left Jona safe at home with our sixteen-year-old neighbor (I thought) while I attended a day-long seminar about a half hour away. Understandably, we'd all been required to turn off our cell phones during the seminar, so I felt a little disconnected from Jona but not worried. Jona was having fun with the neighbor girl, who had babysat with her before, and everything seemed normal as could be. Several hours later we were listening to one of the speakers when I don't know how to describe it, but I knew without a doubt in my mind that I had to get home *immediately*, as fast as I could. I was so sure it was urgent that I didn't even start calling the house until I was in my car, racing home, after running out of the seminar without a word to anyone. My panic got worse and worse as I kept calling over and over again and getting nothing but voice mail. I got home to find Jona alone in the house, lying on the sofa, too weak to move and almost delirious with a 104-degree fever. The babysitter had decided to sneak off to the mall with her boyfriend, 'just for an hour or so.' (I took care of her later, don't worry.) I grabbed Jona and got her to the emergency room in record time, and she was hospitalized for six days with viral pneumonia. Once she was settled into her hospital room and her treatment was underway I apologized to her for not being there and for how scared she must have been, being so sick and all alone. I'll never forget this. She said, 'I wasn't alone, Mommy. The man on the ceiling told me I was going to be okay, and he said you were on your way.' She had mentioned the man on the ceiling before, but I assumed she was just playing. After a lot of reading of Sylvia's books, I'm convinced that he was Jona's Spirit Guide, and that he sent the message to my Spirit Guide that I needed to get home in a big hurry. My friends tease me about believing that, but there's not a doubt in my mind, and all I know is, the man on the ceiling kept my daughter company until I could get to her and kept her from being frightened. Thank God for him and for my Guide or whoever saw to it that I got to Jona when I did."

There may be some of you who, despite all evidence to the contrary, don't believe there really are such things as Spirit Guides. I say the same thing to you that I say to those who don't believe in God: "That's okay. Your Spirit Guide believes in you." And your children's Spirit Guides certainly believe in them, and are watching over them and helping them every minute of every day, whether your children are consciously aware of them or not. (Just because I had no clue about my Spirit Guide Francine until I was seven years old doesn't mean she wasn't with me since the moment I was born.) All I ask is that you not discourage your children from keeping the lines of communication open between them and the divine guidance that accompanied them here. We're all entitled to what we believe. Our children are just as entitled to what they know.

Children and Angels

The final decision every spirit makes on the Other Side before coming to earth for another lifetime—after they've chosen their Spirit Guide and after they've written their intricately detailed chart—is the number and kind of Angels who will be assigned especially to them to protect them until they're Home safely again. Yes, it's true, every child on earth, including you when you were born, arrives with their own band of Angels. The more difficult the chart, the higher the number and level of Angels a spirit recruits. I've never seen fewer than two Angels around any child, and I've seen as many as six. And that's not including the whole legion of Angels who vigilantly and perpetually watch over us all, on call, so to speak, for those times when only God's most perfect, sacred army can accomplish the task at hand.

I know it's a common belief, or hope, that living a pure, exceptional, God-centered life here on earth can result in our ascending to the Other Side to become Angels. People are invariably disappointed when I tell them the truth about that, and I want to say again: Please don't be disappointed! It has nothing to do with God loving us any less than He loves Angels, or valuing us less, or feeling we're unworthy of the honor. He loves every one of His creations equally, perfectly, and unconditionally.

The one and only reason that we never have been and never will be Angels is that Angels are simply a different species than we are. We'll never be giraffes or eagles for the same reason. And make no mistake about it, God treasures animals every bit as much as he treasures us and the Angels. In fact, animals' spirits are so much more advanced than ours that they don't reincarnate—they don't need to. But in the eternal journey of the soul, we always remain the same species we were created to be, which makes our becoming an Angel a simple physiological impossibility.

Here's the most obvious distinction between Angels and us: Angels never incarnate. They never experience life in a human body. So by definition anyone in a human body can be ruled out as a past, present, or future Angel.

They do appear on earth in human form, briefly, when circumstances demand. They stay just long enough to accomplish the task at hand and then disappear again, as described perfectly in a recent letter from Dyanne:

"We were on a family vacation on the Jersey shore, my husband and three children and me. My children are all good swimmers, so we felt safe letting them play and swim in the ocean close to the crowded beach. Suddenly an undertow grabbed hold of my eight-year-old son, Mac, and pulled him under and away from the rest of us. I don't remember much about the next several minutes beyond a lot of panic and a lot of yelling and people trying to get to him. What I do remember as if it just happened a minute ago was the sight of what I assumed was a lifeguard emerging from the water with Mac in his arms. He carried my son to the beach and laid him down on a towel on the sand while a crowd gathered around. Mac coughed up a lot of water, and he was shaken up, but he was breathing fine and sitting up in no time. As soon as I knew my son was okay I turned around to thank this heroic stranger who had saved his life. He was nowhere to be found. He wasn't among the crowd of people, he wasn't anywhere on the long stretches of beach all around us, he was just *gone*. Other people started looking for him too, but we never saw him again. No one remembered seeing him before the accident either, and no one knew who he was, including the lifeguards. He was tall and muscular, very handsome almost to the point of being pretty, and his skin was a kind of tawny color that kind of glistened, which I thought at the time was because he was wet. But when I looked back on it I realized we were all wet and no one else's skin seemed to sparkle like that as if it had a fine dusting of glitter all over it. Also looking back I realized that throughout the whole thing, he never said a word. I'm not writing to ask if this was an Angel. I know it was. My heart knows it was, and I thank God every day for sending him to save my son."

I hate to use the word *typical* when it comes to beings as sacred as Angels, but that story is a classic, typical Angel intervention on earth, in several ways:

* When Angels appear on earth in human form, the encounter is always relatively brief, and the Angel seems to appear out of nowhere and then vanish again just as quickly.

* In their eternal lives as Angels, they're androgynous. Their species is not divided into male and female as ours is. Their bodies will appear to be one or the other when they take human form, but only to attract as little attention as possible. Their faces, on the other hand, are all identical and all exquisite. "Handsome almost to the point of being pretty" is an apt description—not a man's facial features or a woman's, just perfect and unforgettably beautiful. And they assume any human form that will make them inconspicuous, any age at all, any wardrobe that will allow them to fit into a crisis situation without becoming its focal point. The

Bible, in Hebrews, chapter 13, verse 2, illustrates this chameleon aspect far better than I can: "Be not forgetful to entertain strangers, for thereby some have entertained Angels unaware."

*   There are no discernible races among the vast legion of Angels. Both in their brief visits in human form and out of disguise in their natural form, they transcend race. Their skin color is invariably described as simply tawny, or golden brown or tan. But those who've had encounters with Angels are invariably almost too fixated on another consistent feature of the Angels' skin to pay much attention to the color: You'll rarely hear anyone talk about an Angel without commenting on the fact that its skin seemed to sparkle or glitter, as if the sun is perpetually glistening off of it. Again, that's true whether the Angel is appearing as a human or as itself. They do have a subtle glow, created from within by the pure white light of the Holy Spirit, God's sacred energy that forms their very essence and leaves the finest residue of divine illumination on their skin.

*   Angels never, ever speak. Their communication is exclusively telepathic. (You'll read more about telepathy in Chapter Seven.) And their telepathic communication is so powerful that it often doesn't occur to those who've encountered Angels on earth until later that the Angel actually never said a word. This isn't to imply that Angels don't have voices. They do—voices so exquisite that there aren't words in any human language to describe them. But Angels' voices are only heard in choruses of celebration for the glory of

God, hymns so transcendently soaring that they once pierced the veil between earth and the Other Side to announce and sanctify the birth of the baby Jesus.

Teaching your children everything there is to know about Angels is one of the greatest gifts you can give them, a gift that will bring them comfort and hope throughout their lives but will also help them (and you) understand the magnificent array of heavenly visitors who are drawn to children like moths to flames. Children, as we know, are among the purest, most spiritually conscious beings on earth, rivaled only by animals, and it's a fact worth remembering in your own life that the more spiritually open and available we become, the more Angels gather around us.

One of the most charming stories you'll ever read about a tiny child's awareness of Angels with no effort to exaggerate or impress came from Keith about his two-year-old son, Tommy. "We were sitting at the dinner table one night and Tommy started waving his hands around his head like he was swatting something away, saying, 'No, stop it, don't!' We asked him what was wrong, and he said there were bees all around him. Well, we couldn't see anything around him, let alone bees, so we explained that bees live outdoors, not indoors, and we were sure they would go back outside where they belonged if he just ignored them. He was very annoyed with us that we didn't do anything to make the bees go away. Not long after that I was reading to him from a book that had pictures of Angels in it. He gasped, pointed to one of the pictures and said, "Daddy, look! Bees!"

Of the thousands of letters and client stories I've read and heard about children's encounters with Angels, not one has included the child being frightened or running away as they sometimes do when a spirit appears. Angels are so sacred, so perfect, and such a direct link to God Himself that fear in their presence is an impossibility. And unlike Spirit Guides, Angels don't advise us, read our charts, or urge us in one direction or another through earthly lives they've never experienced and can't possibly relate to. There's a divine purity to their purpose in our lives: They are our holiest, most powerful protectors.

There are actually eight levels of Angels. These eight levels have nothing to do with status; they simply designate the body of experience an Angel has accumulated in its eternal lifetime. As Angels acquire more experience in their divine work as messengers, protectors, and miracle workers, they ascend to higher levels. No Angel is valued less than any other by their Creator. They simply amass more and more power as they achieve higher and higher levels.

To help children know which level of Angel they're seeing around them, tell them to watch closely to see what color the Angels' wings are, since that's how one level is physically distinguished from another when Angels are at Home on the Other Side.

First, there are the least experienced ones, simply called Angels, whose wings are a dusty gray white.

Next come the Archangels, with pure white wings.

The Cherubim are next. Their wings are white with gold tips.

The Cherubim are followed by the Seraphim. Their wings are white with silver tips.

Then come the Virtues, with their pale blue wings, followed by the Dominions, with green wings.

The second highest level of Angels are the Thrones, whose wings are a deep, royal purple.

Last come the highest level, the most powerful Angels of all.

They're called the Principalities, and their wings are a brilliant solid gold.

Not only do children appreciate and enjoy watching for Angels with different-colored wings, but there's a valuable piece of information for them, and you, to keep in mind about the distinction between the levels. The first seven levels, from the Angels to the Thrones, can take the initiative to descend to our sides whenever and wherever they're needed. Whether God sends them or they perceive the crisis themselves, they can intervene on our behalf in less time than the single beat of a heart.

The Principalities, on the other hand, powerful beyond our ability to imagine, only come to us under two circumstances: Either God commands them to our rescue, or we specifically call for them in the most dire emergencies. The Principalities can create miracles. They can bring even the most lost of souls back to God-centered faith, health, and sobriety. And they can, in the most awesome, seemingly impossible feats of strength, speed, and humanity, save lives.

"I'm twenty-four years old now," wrote Lawrence, "but something happened to me when I was six that I will never forget and that gives me faith that God really does watch over us. I was on the school playground for recess when a car went out of control and crashed through the chain link fence right into the playground. Everyone was running and screaming and going crazy. I was playing right by the fence, so the car was speeding right at me. I started to run too, but all of a sudden I noticed a bright light right behind me. I didn't know what it was or why it was there, and I didn't have time to turn around to look before I felt something give me a hard push out of the way of the car. The push knocked me down on the ground, and I still remember lying there on my stomach with whatever this light was lying on top of me holding me down and protecting me until the car had stopped with its left front tire about two feet away from my legs. When I stood up just a few seconds later the light was gone, and I looked around to see everyone staring at me from several yards away. No one was anywhere even close by who could possibly have pushed me out of the way of that car and then shielded me while I was lying there, and when I asked my classmates and teachers what they saw, they said it was like an invisible Superman almost picked me up and threw me on the ground in the nick of time. Except that most of them saw the light too, they just couldn't see what was causing it. I don't even need to ask you if it was an Angel who saved my life, Sylvia. I know it was, and I still thank God every day for it, all these years later."

That Angel was one of the Principalities, and the light so many saw was the glow of its golden wings. Another of the Principalities was there for a four-year-old girl named Carrie just a short time ago. Her mother, Diane, wrote, "It had been raining nonstop for two days, so when there was finally a break in the clouds my daughter Carrie couldn't get outside fast enough to ride her new bike on the semicircular driveway in front of our house. I was watching out the window when a big work van came speeding around the corner, lost control on the wet street, and jumped the curb, headed straight for my daughter who was just a few feet away. I flew out of the house, but somehow before I could get to her she seemed to almost float off her bike and land off to the side, safe and sound. In the meantime, the van screeched to a stop on top of Carrie's bike, totally destroying it. I ran to Carrie, and she threw her arms around my neck and said, 'Did you see the Angel, Mama?' I asked her what Angel, what was she talking about, and she said, 'The Angel who lifted me off my bike so I wouldn't die.' Carrie was crying as she told me about the Angel, but they were tears of joy, not fear, and I felt very humble that my own little angel was given a miracle."

Henry told a story that made me smile—not only had his son Jay been seeing his Angel all his life, but his Angel had become a familiar enough presence to warrant Jay's naming him Ball (Jay's favorite toy). And Ball, Jay's Angel, was still his constant sidekick by the time Jay was six years old and had stopped being able to see other visitors from the spirit world who'd been a routine part of his life when he was a toddler. As Henry told it, "We were on a family trip. I was driving, my wife was in the passenger seat, and Jay was in the back seat behind me. A car appeared from a side road, coming right at us, moving so fast there was nothing I could do. I knew that car was going to hit my door, and worse, my son's door, head on, and all I could do was yell, 'Jay! Get down!' Crazy as it sounds, I saw with my own eyes what looked almost like time stood still—the other car seemed to go into slow motion, I don't know any other way to describe it, and it ended up hitting the front left wheel well of our car as if it glided into us instead of slamming into us. Except for a quick jolt, we barely felt a thing inside the car. I immediately turned around to check on Jay and saw him staring out the window with a look of awe on his face, completely uninjured. He later told my wife and me that he saw Ball fly from the back seat beside him to the front of our car, push our car back and then stand there so the other car would hit him instead of us. He was afraid at first that Ball might be hurt, but 'it turns out that Angels can't get hurt that bad,' and, in fact, Ball was just fine."

And then there was the day that one of the Principalities intervened in the lives of my own family. I was in New York to tape *The*

Montel Williams Show. My son Chris, my daughter-in-law Gina, and my then two-year-old granddaughter Angelia were on the trip with me. Chris and I were already at the studio, while Gina was meeting us there after she and Angelia went shopping.

The instant Gina and Angelia appeared at my dressing room door Chris and I knew something shocking had happened. Gina was pale and trembling. Tears were streaming down her face, and she could barely talk. Angelia, in the meantime, was happy as ever as Chris lifted her out of her stroller, thrilled to see her daddy and her Bagdah after a whole hour of being separated from us. When Gina had collected herself again she explained what had so deeply shaken her, and there was as much awe as fear and relief in her voice.

"We were crossing the street a block from here," she said. "We had a green light and the walk sign, but you know me, I still looked before I started across. I'd taken maybe three steps off the curb, pushing Angelia in her stroller, when, as crazy as this sounds, it was like a pair of invisible hands shoved me as hard as they could back onto the curb. I was holding onto Angelia's stroller, obviously, so she kind of flew backward with me, just as a car came screaming past us, right through the light, and right where Angelia was before I got pushed out of the way." Then she looked at me and added, "There was no one around to push me like that, Mom. And if I hadn't been pushed, that car would have killed Angelia. It's that simple. It was an Angel. There's no other explanation. An Angel saved our little girl."

Not every encounter between children and Angels involves a crisis. In fact, like spirits, Angels are around all of us all the time, and children are simply more finely tuned than most adults to that dimension they just left, the Other Side, where Angels live.

This might be a good time to add that not all children see Angels, and not for a minute do I want you to assume it's an indication that there are no Angels surrounding them. I was a psychic child myself, and I didn't actually see the full-blown magnificence of an Angel until I was in my early sixties. I was spending the night at my son Chris's house and got up very early in the morning to get a drink of water. I headed for the stairway in the foyer, a massive space with a thirty-foot-tall ceiling, and literally froze in place, gasping in awe at the top of the stairs, as I found myself in the presence of a glorious, impossibly beautiful Angel, so huge that it filled every inch of the foyer. It was radiant, glowing with God's divine light, and its wings were at full span, pure white with silver tips. One of the Cherubim, standing watch over Angelia, who was sick, and I will always count that moment as one of the most blessed, sacred, humbling events of my life. So please be assured that Angels are with us whether we see them or not, and if you missed out on witnessing them when you were a psychic child (and never forget—you were), there still might be a sighting in your future when you least expect it, no matter what your age.

In the meantime, though, keep an eye on your children and don't let the disadvantages of being a grown-up on earth prevent you from sharing their wonder when Angels reveal themselves.

"Let me start by saying I've never been a believer in spirits, Angels, and the like," Ilene warned. "But I personally witnessed something that turned my whole life around (and it needed it), thanks to my youngest daughter Bree, who's four years old. I'm a single mother of three girls, and they help out with chores around the house. One night just as the sun was going down Bree insisted it was her turn to carry out the trash, which I'd never let her do before because it was heavy for her. I watched from the window to make sure she made it to the trash bin okay. She did, and then instead of coming right back inside she just stood there by the bin looking up at something with the most amazed look on her face. I couldn't imagine what she thought she was seeing, but I could make out a faint white glow of light beside her. She held out her hand for a few seconds, stared at her hand as if she was holding something, and then came racing back into the house, so excited, asking if I'd seen the Angel! I saw that glow of light, but I wasn't about to exaggerate it to the point of being an Angel, and I'm sorry to say I told her I watched her the whole time and there was no Angel out there with her, period. She told me there was too, an Angel in bright white robes, with a ball of light in his hand, and 'he even let me hold the light.' Then she held out her hand to show me, and the whole palm of her hand was covered with what looked like tiny white grains of sand that were sparkling so much I could easily see them without even turning on the porch light. 'He said to tell you everything will be okay, Mama,' she said. I still get tears in my eyes remembering it. Between that glittering sand in her little hand and her little voice comforting me, I was just undone! And it was five days before those sparkles disappeared, as if they were under her skin. A week after that Angel visit I was hired for a good job I had applied for almost two months earlier, which made all the difference in the world financially and really did make everything okay. I want you to know that I apologized to my daughter and told her her mommy was wrong, she did have a visit from an Angel, and I meant every word."

Kelli wrote, "My son Ryan wasn't two years old yet and just barely starting to talk. He was supposed to be taking a nap in his crib, but I heard him giggling hysterically, so I went into the nursery to quiet him down and to find out what was so hilarious. He was squirming all over the place, with his arms waving in the air like he was trying to push something away but not trying very hard. I asked him what was going on, and in the middle of his giggling he got out the words, "Tickling me." I said, 'Who's tickling you?' and he said, 'Angels.' I didn't believe a word of that, not even when I reached into his crib to pick him up and noticed that the air right above him was cold, like there was an air conditioner running at full blast just in that one spot. But then a couple of hours later I was cleaning Ryan's room. I get teased about being a 'clean freak,' and I vacuum and dust in there every day, so I can tell you this wasn't there the day before: On top of his books and shelves that are safely high up on one wall I found a very fine white sparkling film of dust. It was almost like glittering white baby powder, but I never change him in his room and there's never been baby powder in there. None of his toys could possibly have caused it, and I even checked the ceiling vents, but there was no sparkling white dust on those either. I told my sister, who's a total skeptic, and showed her the dust. Even she agreed that Ryan's too young to make up being tickled by Angels and that she'd never seen anything quite like that soft sparkling dust either. We both have come to believe that there were Angels in my son's room, because we can't come up with any other explanation, as crazy as I know that sounds."

Dimitra had a beautifully comforting experience regarding her grandmother Maude, thanks to her three-year-old daughter, Nikki. Maude was terminally ill and had come to live out the last weeks of her life with Dimitra's family. "I'd brought my dear granny her dinner, and even though she didn't touch it when I put the tray in front of her, I'll always remember how peaceful she was when she smiled up at me and whispered, 'Thank you.' Then I went into my daughter's bedroom next to Granny's to check on her. We were lying on her bed playing and talking. The blinds on her big picture window were still open so we could see the beautiful sunset. All of a sudden Nikki's eyes got huge as saucers as she looked out the window, and she let out a gasp. Then she said, 'Mama, look! They here! They so beautiful!' (She wasn't pronouncing her *r*'s very well yet, so 'they're' came out as 'they.') I couldn't see a thing, so I asked her who 'they' were. She said, 'The Angels, Mama. See?' She pointed to the window and then excitedly ran to it, but I still couldn't see anything. I asked Nikki what the Angels were doing, and she said, 'They here for Mamaw (her nickname for my granny).' I couldn't believe it, but I couldn't not believe it either, and I couldn't resist going back into Granny's room. I was shocked and heartbroken and amazed that in the maybe ten minutes since I'd left her, she'd slipped away. There's not a doubt in my mind that my granny's Angels came to take her safely to heaven, and that my innocent three-year-old who'd never heard of Angels that I knew of (I'm ashamed to say) was given the special blessing of seeing them arrive."

And a very interesting point was raised by Lee, who shared a lovely story about his son Evan. "The first time this happened we were on our way to meet my parents for a day of boating on the lake. We were driving along listening to music when suddenly our two-year-old son, Evan, started yelling, 'Angels! See all the Angels!' from his car seat behind my wife. He was very excited, and we looked to see him pointing out the window to his right. To our surprise, he was pointing at the cemetery we happened to be passing, and he didn't calm down again until he couldn't see the cemetery anymore. Of course, we didn't see any Angels, and we wrote it off as just a really odd experience. But since then, I kid you not, no matter how far away from home we travel, and with me and my wife going out of our way not to comment or even glance back at Evan whenever we pass a cemetery, we can count on Evan to become excited again and start yelling at us again to look at all the Angels. It happens too reliably to be a coincidence, and we've stopped having the slightest doubt that our son sees Angels at every cemetery. We were just wondering, if the spirits of all those people who are buried there have passed on to the Other Side, why are there so many Angels hanging around?"

It's an excellent question, and there are actually two reasons you'll find Angels at cemeteries. One is that they're there for the earthbounds who are buried there, those poor confused souls who haven't yet realized they're dead and who need the protection of Angels more than ever until they've safely made it Home again. The other is that Angels flock to cemeteries not for those who've gone to the Other Side but for those who are left behind to grieve and search for comfort at their loved ones' grave sites.

So if you're someone who visits a cemetery to feel some connection to a departed loved one who probably rode there with you and will ride back home with you again, never doubt that as you kneel at the grave, God's most sacred, powerful legion is gathered around you, great wings spread to protect you and wrap you in the arms of His perfect love and healing white light as you make your way through the darkness of grief, lost but never, ever alone.

Orbs

"For as long as I can remember," Wilson wrote, "my son Robbie, who's now seven years old, has been seeing what he describes as 'little round flying things' in the air. He says they're see-through but that they're full of 'a hundred colors.' Sometimes they move very slowly and just seem to float, and other times they zoom around all over the house. And just when it looks like they're going to hit someone, they fly right through them instead as if they're not even there."

Marion reported, "I've taken dozens of photos of my daughter Kelsey since she was born three and a half years ago. I've used several different cameras, most of them glareproof. I've taken indoor photos with and without a flash and outdoor photos with and without a flash at all times of day and night, at our house, at Kelsey's grandparents' houses, at the playground and throughout our cross-country trip to California. And I'd say that in about 80 percent of the photos, there are small balls of lights, like orbs, hovering around Kelsey's head. Some of the orbs are bigger than others, some of them are white, and some of them look multicolored. Since I don't understand what they are and don't want to frighten my daughter, I've just put these photos in our family albums without commenting on them to her. But now she's starting to say she sees them around her in 'real life.' She doesn't seem upset by them, and she seems surprised that I can't see them. When she asks me what they are I tell her in all honesty that I don't know but I'm sure they're not here to hurt her. Sylvia, can you explain what these orbs are and solve what's becoming a major ongoing family mystery?"

My files are filled with letters, e-mails, and photographs concerning children surrounded by orbs. I've read all the same explanations about them that you have, from alien beings, to light refraction that by all laws of physics could never happen, to malfunctioning cameras (or film or processing), to parents indulging children's silly fantasies.

But the truth behind what orbs are is really no more complicated than this: Orbs, no matter what size or color, live or on film (with the exception of countless hoaxes, which I'm always delighted to expose), are nothing less than another way that Angels manifest themselves on earth. Orbs are the intensely concentrated energy of God's most sacred messengers and protectors, glowing from the white light of the Holy Spirit that forms their very essence, and varying in color just as the wings of Angels do, especially when earthly sunlight and moonlight filter through them. Orbs fly and hover and soar as Angels do in their full-blown winged magnificence, and just as you'll find that children are never frightened when Angels appear, you'll also notice that these fairly common glowing balls of light, seemingly inexplicable and mysterious, never frighten them either, because they know when God's purest expressions of love are around them, no matter what form they take.

So the next time your child experiences orbs in their presence, or you happen to see them yourselves or catch them on film, don't overcomplicate one of the simplest, most divine encounters we humans can experience. Just stop to bask in the blessing of His glorious gift and thank Him for loving your child enough to surround them with His Angels.

Children and Totems

When we write our meticulously detailed charts on the Other Side before coming to earth for another lifetime, as you know from your own lives, we don't make it easy on ourselves. If we wanted peace, bliss, and perfection, we'd stay Home. Instead, intent on the continuing growth and Godliness of our spirits, we construct obstacles for our lives on earth to guarantee that we'll accomplish our specific goals while we're here. By choice we'll experience heartache, illness, grief, sorrow, poor choices, failure, fear, and any number of other challenges as we make our way through this tough school we're attending, but to repeat a quote of my Spirit Guide Francine's, "What have you learned when times were good?"

God would never allow us to set out on this overwhelming journey without an army of protection around us. So by His design, we recruit that army from the Other Side to be with us every step of the way while we're gone. We've discussed the Spirit Guides we recruit, and we've discussed our Angels. What we haven't discussed is the other sacred, essential element of our chosen team: our totem.

Our totem is whatever glorious spirit member of the animal kingdom we choose to be our loyal, constant companion away from Home, to stand guard over us, with its pure heart committed solely to our well-being throughout our lifetimes on earth, from our birth until the moment we return to the Other Side. Animals are among God's most divine creations, incarnating just once, for our benefit, but never having to reincarnate because their souls have already achieved perfection. We would never consider leaving the Other Side without our totem, and along with every pet we've ever owned in all our lifetimes on earth, our totem is one of the first to greet us when we arrive safely back Home again.

From time to time I run across someone who refuses to believe they have a totem because they think they don't like animals. If you're among that minority, I can promise you that if you're here from the Other Side you arrived with a chart, and if you arrived with a chart you have a totem. To deny the sanctity of animals in God's eyes is to deny one of the great sources of loyalty and protection you brought with you from Home.

Because totems are part of the spirit world, it's no surprise that children frequently see their own totems. It's also no surprise that it can be a frightening experience for them. We don't always choose totems that are thought of as ferocious. My totem is an elephant, for example, and I have a close friend whose totem is a pig. (My house is filled with tiny elephant replicas, by the way, and my friend has collected every ceramic and toy pig he can get his hands on all his life without knowing why until I explained it to him.) But of course some totems are animals traditionally perceived as dangerous—they are here to protect us, after all. And since our totems have come here for us and us alone, they're fiercely loyal and insist on being right beside us at all times. Children who don't understand what totems are can easily believe that they're being chased by a terrifying animal who might even be growling and baring its teeth, when in reality they're being followed by their bravest, most loving defender who's growling and baring its teeth on the child's behalf, to warn away anyone or anything who might do them harm.

Sheila wrote, "My son Connor has been a happy child since the day he was born, with an ability to see and talk to spirits around him as if it's the most normal thing in the world, not scary at all. But shortly after he turned four, he came screaming into our room in the middle of the night, terrified, sobbing, saying 'the wolf' was after him. We assumed it was a nightmare but we went through the motions of searching his room to prove that there was no wolf in there. He was sure the wolf would come back if we left him alone, so we let him sleep with us that night and felt sure this 'crisis' would be over with by morning. We were wrong. The 'wolf' began showing up at day care and scaring him to the point where on two different occasions I was called away from work to come pick him up. I've given up trying to tell him there's no wolf, because he's convinced there is, and starting trying to tell him the wolf won't hurt him and is just trying to make friends, and that seems to have helped. One day he told me the wolf let Evan pet him on the head. I'm glad things have calmed down and the wolf isn't so scary to my son, but it still doesn't explain why he suddenly started believing a growling wolf was chasing him."

I've got files full of virtually identical letters from deeply concerned parents in which their children are suddenly being terrorized by everything from bears to huge brown cats (a cheetah in one case, a lion in many others) to rhinoceroses to seemingly wild horses. Which is why I can't urge you strongly enough to teach your children about their totems. While a child is still struggling to tell the difference between the spirit world and the earthly one, it couldn't be more natural that they don't always recognize their totems as spirit animals whose sole, noble purpose is to stay by their side and, with all their ferocity, protect them from spiritual harm. When it comes to totems, I promise you, it couldn't be safer, and more helpful to your children, to encourage them to stop running, let their totem catch them, and make friends. And if, in the process, your child learns to love earthly animals as well, all of whom will become totems themselves someday, so much the better.

Children and Azna, the Mother God

We all know that there is a Father God, omnipotent, perfect, all loving and all knowing.

There is also a Mother God. Her name is Azna. She is the counterpart of the Father, worshipped by religions around the world for more than twenty thousand years.

The Father God is the intellect of creation, unchanging, all loving and omnipotent. Azna, the Mother God, is His complement, creation's equally loving and omnipotent emotion. She can move, nurture, and intervene. The relationship between Azna and earth is an intimate one, since earth is the most emotionally motivated of all the inhabited planets, and she's historically taken form among us to create miracles, as she did at Lourdes, Fatima, and Guadalupe. Whether she's called the Blessed Mother, the Lady of Lotus, Ashara, Theodora, Sophie, or Isis by the many faiths who adore her, the Mother God is the harmonizer, the activist, the keeper of life. Her dominion is all living things on earth, and the icon of Mother Nature was inspired by her powerful unconditional love for everything on this planet that lives and struggles to thrive in spite of humankind's abuse and oblivion.

Without the intellect we genetically inherited from the Father God, we would be pure emotion. Without Azna, we would be pure intellect, unable to connect to our inherent empathy that tells our souls when a hand needs to be held or a comforting hug offered.

Azna has been worshipped since the ancient Greeks, who called her Earth Gaea, the Mother Goddess who brought forth the sky, the mountains, and the sea. Plato wrote of her in 415 B.C., calling her

Ge. The Romans revered her by the name of Terra Mater, the Mother of Earth.

And then along came Western religion, and Christianity in particular, which, gorgeous as it is in countless ways—and I myself am a Gnostic Christian, so believe me, no one loves our Lord more than I—was determined to be a patriarchy. Eve, the first woman, for example, was the second human to be created, from Adam's rib, according to the Bible, as if she was simply an extension of him. Eve's primary legacy seems to be the introduction of sin into the paradise of the Garden of Eden. In a patriarchal religion, there was no use for a Mother God. Mind you, everywhere you look throughout creation there is duality—good and evil, day and night, black and white, yin and yang—and the Bible reminds us that the universe was created in His image. So to suggest that God Himself isn't a duality is to overlook a key element in what the Bible says is the essence of Him.

It's Azna whose exquisite materialized presence is the last we see before we leave the Other Side for another incarnation on earth. It's Azna who hears our prayers right along with the Father God, and who feels all the more sanctified when our prayers are directed to Her. Even if believing in Her is hard, or contrary to your upbringing, offer Her a specific prayer of thanks from time to time and ask for some small gesture from Her, if only out of curiosity—an unexpected call from an old friend, an apology from someone who's hurt your feelings, an act of kindness from a stranger when you're having a bad day, something specific that will catch your attention. Your belief in Her is not a condition of Her generosity. Like her counterpart, the Father God, Azna adores you, and she finds Her joy in your spirit's greatest happiness.

As the emotional, nurturing half of the Godhead, the Mother

God has an intimate, hands-on relationship with children. She appears most often to children, as she did at Fatima, Lourdes, and Guadalupe, and as she may appear to your children as well, in private moments, less celebrated but no less miraculous, to remind them that with every breath, they're surrounded by perfect love and nurtured by the promise of eternity.

"My three-year-old daughter Kitty was in the hospital, running a dangerously high fever, weak and sick as she could be," wrote Stacie. "The doctors were giving her every test they could think of to find out what was wrong and what to do about it, but they were having no luck. I was trying to get some sleep one night in the chair beside her bed when I was startled to see Kitty sit up on her own for the first time in days. She was staring at something at the foot of her bed. Her eyes were wide open, and she was wide awake. I went to her and asked her what she was looking at, but she didn't even seem to know I was in the room until she lay back down after a minute or two of staring. Then she looked at me, and she was smiling. She distinctly said, 'Pretty lady, Mommy. Yellow hair. I be okay.' I put my hand on her forehead just to comfort her and brush back her hair, and I couldn't believe it—for the first time in almost a week, her forehead was cool. Her fever had broken. I ran out and got the night nurse, who confirmed that Kitty's temperature was normal again and she was out of the woods. When I told the nurse what had happened, she explained that it's not uncommon for children with high fevers to hallucinate like that. What she couldn't explain is how a hallucination broke my little girl's fever. No one will ever convince me that the Blessed Mother didn't come to my daughter that night and heal her."

Multiply that letter by thousands and thousands and you'll have some idea of the stories I've heard over the years of Azna's special visits to children around the world. Whether they're ill, or lonely, or frightened, or Homesick, or simply in need of a moment of divine attention, children see Azna or simply feel Her presence, even if they're not consciously aware of Her, and their spirits are graced and nourished by the Mother God.

In the next chapter you'll read about the many trips children (and all of us, for that matter) take to the Other Side while they sleep. When my granddaughter Angelia was a little girl, she retained her memories of those trips when she was awake, and she told me about seeing the cherished statue of Azna that stands at the entrance to a building called the Hall of Justice. Unbeknown to me until then, she'd also had a personal visitation from Mother God. As if it was the most interesting part of the story, she commented that, "In real life she has curls on top of her head, but in the statue she has her hair long."

Listen and learn from your children's stories about a beautiful woman whose yellow hair is either long or in curls on top of her head. Teach them about Azna, and teach them to pray to both their Mother and Father God. Then watch as the special blessings and the added peace of their Nurturer begin to flow.

CHAPTER SIX

While Children Sleep

When my son Chris was three years old, I started asking him every morning if he slept well and if he'd had any dreams during the night. Several times a week he'd answer that he dreamed he was playing with his friends on the steps of a great big white building. I'd encourage him to tell me more, but he didn't seem to find it all that interesting—it was always just friends, playing on steps, great big white building and, "What's for breakfast?"

This went on for a few weeks. Looking back, I'm surprised at myself for being so dense about what was going on, and it took my Spirit Guide Francine to point it out. One morning, after yet another report from Chris about the same supposed dream, Francine had a little talk with me about Chris's nighttime activities. It seemed that he and a group of other children from earth were routinely gathering on the steps of the Hall of Wisdom, one of the most gorgeous and revered buildings on the Other Side, to play, giggle, and chase each other around. It would be greatly appreciated by the general population of Home, she said, if I would ask Chris to please either play more quietly or find a more appropriate place to get together with his friends.

I had a talk with Chris, who seemed to understand exactly what I was talking about, and there was never another complaint from the Other Side about his disruptive behavior when he went Home during the night to visit.

All sorts of magic happens when children sleep and their spirits are left to their own devices, unsupervised and unencumbered by their conscious minds. The various forms that magic takes have been explored by countless researchers and resulted in countless written studies. Unfortunately, the vast majority of those studies are based on the incorrect premise that children arrive here brand new, as clean slates with no past at all. Of course, the truth is that every child arrives with a spirit that always was and always will be, with wisdom and memories from past incarnations and from their full, busy lives on the Other Side. They've come from the perfection of Home to the imperfection of life on earth. They've come from the complete freedom of movement of the spirit world to the limitations of physical bodies and gravity. And they've recently been through the trauma of being born, which I've learned through countless regressive hypnosis sessions makes the trauma of dying look like a stroll in the park. Yes, they've come here by their own choice, just as we all have. But just because it's voluntary doesn't mean it's easy, and any enlisted soldier going through boot camp will back me up on that.

You know that much of what goes on with you while you sleep involves various forms of working through what's happening in your life, what's been happening in your recent past, and what you're hoping might (or might not) be happening in your future. Exactly the same is true while children sleep, and that makes complete sense if you keep in mind that their recent past involves the perfection of Home and the previous lives that are still fresh in their spirit consciousness. In their current lives they're dealing with cell memories triggered by being in a body again, they're surrounded by strangers, their vocabularies are limited, the language being spoken all around them is completely foreign, and they're well aware of how physically vulnerable and defenseless they are. It's a lot to work through in the course of a night's sleep.

The Complexity of Children's Dreams

According to several formal studies, prior to age three or four, children never include themselves in their dreams. That's very true. Why? Because in entering these brand new incarnations, they haven't yet developed any sense of exactly who they are. Their personas on the Other Side are familiar to them, and their identities in past lives are still relatively fresh in their minds. But for their first handful of years this time around, they're struggling to fit the seemingly disjointed, unfamiliar pieces of the puzzle of their new life into the bigger picture of their spirits' eternal journey without the benefit of a solid identity base to work from. I've worked with toddlers who could tell me their names on the Other Side more readily than they could tell me their given names in this lifetime (and yes, we all have names at Home, which remain constant throughout our eternal lives there). I've worked with an equal number of toddlers who could describe previous incarnations in detail more clearly than they could tell me the basics about their current parents and siblings. As long as children are still more comfortable with who they used to be than with who they are now, it's perfectly natural that their current identity wouldn't play a significant role in their dreams.

Studies also show that until they're around six years old, children don't include strangers in their dreams. I've found that to be true as well. Again, why? Because before the age of six, children's spirits while they sleep will gravitate to whatever's most familiar to them, and when they're that young, what's familiar is past lives on earth and at Home and the populations of those lives, and the population of their immediate current vicinity. Even if they don't recognize those past-life friends, family members, and enemies in their conscious minds, you can bet their spirit minds know who they are and weave them into their dreams for the most deliberate, useful reasons.

Just as with us adults, children experience five different categories of dreams. A simple understanding of these five categories and their significance will help you make far more sense of your own dreams. But of far more importance for this discussion, it will help you and your children make sense of, and make friends with, all their nighttime adventures and dreams—yes, even the scary ones. And what a beautiful lifelong gift to give them.

Dream Category #1: Astral Travel

We all know as a fact, not a theory, that our spirits can and do function separately from our bodies. If that weren't true, we wouldn't survive death and live eternally as we know we do, just as God promised. And that fact is the core of the very common phenomenon of astral travel.

Astral travel is nothing more than our spirits taking a break from these earthly bodies they're temporarily housed in and taking off to visit whomever or wherever we want. It's our natural mode of transportation when we're on the gravity-free dimension of Home. It brought us here from the Other Side when we entered the fetus to be born, and it will take us Home again when our bodies give out.

Astral travel is responsible for some of our most vivid and memorable dreams, taking us to meet loved ones from this life and past lives and to visit places we miss—most especially the Other Side, for which we're all Homesick from the moment we leave. In fact, adults astrally travel to the Other Side on an average of two or three times a week while we sleep. For children, who've so recently come from there, the average is more like five or six times a week. The story of my son Chris that started this chapter is a typical example of a child's spirit taking a quick, joyful trip Home while the physical body and conscious mind are conveniently sleeping. And I do mean typical. Whether or not they're able to verbalize it or define exactly where they were, your children are on those same journeys while they sleep, very real journeys that aren't actually dreams at all.

There are a couple of simple ways to tell a child's dream (or yours) from an astral trip:

* If your child dreams they're flying without benefit of an airplane or other external means, it's not a dream. They're astrally traveling. And not all astral trips disguised as dreams involve flying. Astrally traveling to the Other Side comes so naturally to children (and us) that they can instantaneously get there without needing the added sensations of the trip at all.

* Astral travel experiences, unlike dreams, unfold in a logical sequence of events, just as waking experiences do, rather than in a haphazard jumble of images, people, and locations.

165

Once children have left their bodies, they have three speeds of astral travel to choose from. The first speed is the least disorienting—their spirits move at the same pace their bodies do here on earth. The intermediate speed is fast enough to create the illusion that they're standing still while everything around them is flying past them from front to back. Intermediate speed is often accompanied by the sensation of moving against a roaring wind, which is actually not wind at all but their own rapid forward movement instead. At supernormal speed, their spirits can travel incomprehensible distances faster than the conscious, finite mind can imagine, to the point where they might remember where they went and what they did while we visited, but they have no awareness at all of how they got there and how they got back. If your child ever has an uncannily realistic dream of exploring a distant planet or touring a newly discovered galaxy halfway across the universe, you can bet they're not making it up and that they've experienced astral travel at supernormal speed.

One of the most common astral travel experiences children enjoy while they sleep is getting together with the spirit of a deceased loved one—or, in the case of Melina's four-year-old daughter, Lydia, a loved one who's newly free from their body and headed Home. "My ninety-four-year-old father was living with us in a downstairs den we'd converted into a hospital room for him. We all adored him, but my daughter Lydia was the apple of her 'gampy's' eye, and she took it upon herself to 'read' to him every night before she went to bed, which in her case meant sitting beside him and flipping through the pages of her favorite picture books and making up stories as she went along. Early one morning I went downstairs to check on him and discovered sadly that he'd passed away during the night. While my husband dealt with everything that needed to be done, I went to Lydia's room and sat down next to her on her bed. She woke up immediately and looked at me and said, 'Gampy's gone to heaven, Mama.' I was shocked that she told me before I had a chance to say a word, and I asked her how she knew. She said, 'Because we were flying in the night, and he said so. We saw you and Daddy sleeping with the TV.' My husband and I have talked about this a hundred times, and we're 100 percent sure there's no way Lydia could have known that on that one night, and only that one night, my husband forgot to set our TV's sleep timer and the television was on all night, but the volume was set so low that we slept through it. If it was too quiet to keep us awake, my daughter couldn't possibly have heard it all the way down the hall with her door and ours both closed. When she added that 'Gampy says he'll come see us all the time, so don't be sad,' I knew in the bottom of my heart that every word she was saying was true. It brings me more comfort than I have words to express that he really will be around, and that our precious Lydia will probably be the one to tell us all about it."

I particularly love stories about children's astral trips when the information they offer about them can be validated. How else would Lydia have known, except as an eye witness, that her grandfather passed away during the night, or that her parents' TV was on while they slept when that obviously wasn't their habit?

And speaking of 'how else would they have known?' Don sent a wonderful letter about his three-year-old son, Mike's recurring dream: "My mother died ten months before my son Mike was born. She was a very special woman, and I've always been sorry they 'missed' each other, because she'd been looking forward to grandchildren since the day my wife and I got married. One morning shortly after Mikey turned three years old he was excited to tell me that he and his Granny Joan (our name for my mom) were playing together while he was asleep. Needless to say, I assumed he just had a nice dream about her, and I asked him what all they did when they played but only to make conversation. He said they played 'fort' (his favorite game) and then she took him for a ride in her 'funny red car with a horse on it.' I nearly fell off my chair. My mother lived in a retirement complex for several years, and she bought herself a custom-made golf cart to get around while she was there. It was red, with a horse's face and reins painted on the front of it and a long horse's tail on the back. She got the biggest kick out of that cart, but it was long gone by the time she moved to the nursing home where she died. I couldn't believe Mike knew about Granny Joan's red golf cart. I had never talked about it, and my wife didn't know a thing about it. I looked through every picture I own of my mom, and there wasn't a single one of her and her 'funny red car with a horse on it.' I'm telling you, it's impossible for Mike to have found out about it from anyone but his Granny Joan. And while I keep on trying not to let on to my son how amazed I am, he keeps on visiting with his Granny Joan two or three times a week while he sleeps."

I really can't encourage you enough to do exactly what this man did: If there's a doubt in your mind that your child is taking very real astral trips while they sleep, and bringing back information they'd have no other way of knowing, leave no stone unturned trying to come up with any viable, legitimate alternative. You won't find a more enthusiastic believer in validation than me, or a bigger skeptic than me until I've witnessed some kind of validation myself. So while I know your children are astrally traveling during sleep, going Home to see their favorite friends and places, revisiting past lives and spending time with deceased loved ones they may or may not have met on earth, I don't want you to take my word for it. Listen to your child, ask the right questions, and take their word for it instead.

Dream Category #2: Release Dreams

Release dreams are usually the most confusing, chaotic, silly, or disturbing dreams children, and adults, experience. They're also among the most necessary, because it's through release dreams that they'll emotionally exhale whatever anxiety and frustration they're experiencing, and/or simply be entertained by a seemingly haphazard array of images to make them laugh. Release dreams, many of which play out as nightmares, can also help children access and exorcise painful past-life/cell memories, so that despite the temporary fear and discomfort these dreams might cause, they provide some much-needed healing in the long run. As with the release dreams of adults, children's release dreams don't occur for the purpose of any particular spiritual growth. Instead, they act as safety valves, letting off the mental, emotional, and physiological steam that's inevitable in the course of our difficult lives on earth.

You might be wondering how much anxiety and frustration a small child can go through, with their needs taken care of and no responsibilities to deal with beyond eating, sleeping, and playing. Again, please remember where they've come from—a trip from one dimension to another, and from perfect God-centered bliss surrounded by happy, loving spirits to this imperfect world full of strangers. And never underestimate the physical and emotional trauma of being born, which is also a part of their recent memories. So yes, there's plenty of anxiety in even the most pampered child's life as they adjust to their new lifetime here, and plenty of frustration as their spirits find themselves confined in a physical, gravity-challenged body again.

"Our daughter Jamie has had dreams since she was about three years old, maybe younger, that seem to terrify her," wrote Mary, "and they all seem to involve waking up and finding herself all alone in an empty house. She thinks we've moved, or gone away somewhere without her, and it breaks her heart. It breaks my heart too, that even in a dream she could imagine such a thing and go through so much fear and sadness before she wakes up 'for real' and sees that it didn't really happen."

That may be one of the most common release dreams a child experiences: varying expressions of their fear of abandonment. Part of that comes from their awareness that they're housed in tiny, defenseless bodies and incapable of taking care of themselves. But a much larger part of it is that, even though they're here by their own choice, as we all are, they're suddenly no longer surrounded by everyone and everything they recognize, trust, and love. How could they not feel abandoned? All the love and attention and affection you can surround them with are essential in helping them through it, obviously. But their release dreams help as well, painful as they are temporarily, to work through an emotional transition they have no way of expressing, to themselves or to us, while they're awake.

Think about your own release dreams. What the darkest ones boil down to is a demonstration of our idea of a worst-case scenario, some version of the most awful thing we can possibly imagine in areas of our lives that matter to us. We usually refuse to let our conscious minds fantasize such awful things for more than a second before we force those thoughts right out of our head. But what our conscious minds push away, our subconscious minds keep track of and act out, ultimately to reassure us that even if our version of the worst happens, we'll somehow manage to survive it, emotionally devastating as it might be. It's normal and human that awake or asleep, no matter what the circumstance, we need to believe that somehow, in the long run, we'll be okay, and release dreams give us the opportunity to act out various scenarios and experience surviving them. Hard as it might be to realize when we first wake up from upsetting release dreams, they're worth being grateful for.

I want you to learn that lesson and take it to heart, if for no other reason than to teach it to your child. With their own imagery and the complicated issues we've discussed, their release dreams are as essential to their well-being as yours are to you, and the more you help them appreciate rather than fear those dreams the more peace of mind you're giving them, not just throughout their childhood but for the rest of their life.

Dream Category #3: Wish Dreams

Just as children express their fears, frustrations, and confusion in their dreams, they also express their hopes and wishes. Wish dreams are exactly what they sound like—sweet, lovely reflections of what children want.

Some of their wish dreams are simple and literal. They love horses, they dream of getting a pony. They're fascinated with trains, they dream of being an engineer. They can't get enough of Spiderman, they dream of being a superhero. They're thrilled by baseball, they dream of pitching a perfect game. Straightforward, fun, and informative about your child's interests, so pay attention.

Other wish dreams, though, aren't meant to be taken literally and need to be explored beneath their surface. They can offer valuable insights into a child's less obvious, more internal yearning. And, as you'll see in this letter from Bridget, you might save yourself some hurt feelings if you'll keep gently asking questions until you get past the most superficial interpretation and keep digging.

"My three-year-old son Shawn is a good-natured, easy-going little boy in general, but he woke up even happier than usual one morning last week. I said, 'You must have had sweet dreams to be such a happy guy today.' He nodded, and then he told me that in his dream he was on a big white boat that belonged to his 'real mom and dad' and his 'two brothers' and they were fishing. Then they were in the woods to find a Christmas tree, and then his 'real dad' took him and his 'brothers' for a ride on a real fire truck. He was practically glowing as he told me all this, and he couldn't stop saying how much fun it was. I tried to keep smiling while I listened to him, but in my heart, I was devastated. I like to think we have an ideal family and that we're providing Shawn with as secure and joyful a life as any child could want. But we must be doing something wrong for him to make up a whole other family and life for himself, with his 'real parents' (Shawn is our biological child) and two brothers (Shawn has no brothers, just one sister five years older who loves him to death). Or maybe this is a family from a past life (I strongly believe in past lives) and he'd rather be with them. I feel petty being jealous of either an imaginary family or one that's long gone, but there's no denying that dreaming about these other people put a great big smile on my son's face. If there's something we're doing wrong, or something we should be doing that we're not, I'd appreciate knowing what it is."

First of all, Bridget was right in her guess that this wish dream was a montage of memories of his past-life family. If she had asked questions, Shawn probably would have told her more about them and discovered what I can tell her psychically—they really did live an idyllic life of privilege in Maine, third-generation wealth that allowed the family to enjoy an enormous amount of leisure time together. Shawn and his two brothers were very close in age and inseparable. Bridget, later in her letter, described the family-owned business that she and her husband started a few years before Shawn was born, that was thriving thanks to their hard work and long hours. She also wrote with justifiable pride that owning their own business allowed them the flexibility to participate in carpooling responsibilities and their eight-year-old daughter's many extracurricular activities, from music lessons to gymnastics to dance lessons. And while his parents were at work, Shawn was a few blocks away at his grandparents' house. "He's the joy of their lives, and they're spoiling him rotten, just like grandparents are supposed to do. And every Sunday, no matter what, is Family Day, just us, spending time together."

In other words, these are good people, working hard to provide the best lives possible for their children. What Shawn is missing, and what his wish dream expressed, is simply the luxury of leisure time with his family, and built-in playmates within that family who enjoy the same things he does. It didn't mean that he loved that family from his past life more. It meant that he wishes that he and his current family, whom he loves every bit as much, could relax and play more often together, and that he and his older sister could find more common ground that they could mutually enjoy. Nobody's doing anything wrong, Shawn's certainly not being deprived, and God knows very few of us are wealthy enough to spend the majority of our lives on adventures with our children. So by looking below the surface of Shawn's wish dream, and getting past the mistaken idea that Shawn is yearning for his past-life family, Bridget can find a wonderful compliment: He adores and enjoys the family he's part of now, and his wish is more time with them.

Once you understand your child's wish dreams, both the straightforward literal ones and the ones that require a little more exploring, you'll be amazed at how much they'll tell you about what's on your child's mind and what they hope for during their private sleep time. You'll also be amazed at what a difference it will make to them to have their wishes heard, acknowledged, and respected, whether or not they can be fulfilled.

Dream Category #4: Information and Problem Solving
Dream Category #5: Precognition

These last two categories are hard to separate, because the information in these dreams, whether it's concerned with the present or the future, comes from many of the same sources. We'll be discussing those sources in depth in Chapter Seven, but for now the important thing to remember about all your children's dreams in these categories is this: If the information or predictions your child receives in their dreams turn out to be inaccurate, the dreams were undoubtedly either wish or release dreams. If, on the other hand, they turn out to be accurate, you can rest assured they came from the spirit world and the infinite resources of the Other Side.

"This story still makes the hair on the back of my neck stand up," Gwen wrote, "but it happened, and my husband and I are both witnesses to it. We're blessed with a beautiful three-year-old daughter, Casey. Sweet, bright, fun-loving, and normal as can be. On the morning of April 3 she woke up very sad. I asked what was wrong. Before she could answer me the phone rang. My husband went into the kitchen to answer it, and when Casey and I were alone she said, 'Aunt Tina went to heaven.' (My husband's sister Tina, who was struggling with a severe drug problem.) I asked where she got that idea, since we'd just seen Tina two days before. Casey replied, 'In a dream.' (Or 'dweam,' as she calls it.) Right that second my husband came back from the kitchen, so upset he was shaking. All he said was, 'Tina overdosed last night. She's gone.' I don't know what shocked me more, that Tina had passed away or that Casey knew it before the call came breaking the news to us."

Georgia wrote, "My daughter Lynette isn't even four years old yet and has started having dreams that come true. The latest one was two nights ago when she had a dream that there was an ambulance in our driveway. We're all in good health and have never had to call an ambulance in our sixteen years of marriage and three children. Yesterday my mother-in-law came to stay with us. She forgot to bring her medication and began having seizures. We called 9-1-1, and next thing we knew there was an ambulance in our driveway. I wasn't even smart enough to put it together. It was Lynette who did, when we were watching the paramedics and she said, 'See, Mommy?' "

And this letter came from Anthony: "I was driving my four-year-old son, Patrick, to preschool one morning when he casually announced, 'I'm going to have a baby sister.' I thought he was just playing and making noise, since he's always been a chatterbox, so I said, 'Maybe someday, son, we'll see.' He sounded kind of exasperated with me, like either I was stupid or he didn't appreciate being blown off like that, and told me, 'No, Daddy, she's already here in Mommy's tummy. I saw her while I was asleep.' " I called my wife and told her about it when I got to work. I've always been quicker to dismiss this kind of thing than she is, and by the time I got home that night she'd taken a home pregnancy test and got a positive result. The doctor confirmed a few days later that she was two months pregnant, and six and a half months after that Patrick got his baby sister, Jolene. I'll never forget that, and I'll never understand how he came up with something it was impossible for him to know."

Asleep or awake, children can be especially gifted receivers when it comes to information about the present or future. I made this point in Chapter Three, but it bears repeating now: It always makes me smile to read the amazingly common phrase "impossible for them to know" when adults are commenting on unexpected information children have shared with them. Clearly it's not impossible, let's face it—if they have the information, and if it's accurate, it's not only possible, it's a fact. It's not some mysterious fluke, or something they pull out of thin air (whatever on earth that means), or something researchers occasionally refer to as an area we continue to explore (translation: "We don't have a clue"). The factual information children pick up has its origin in very real, specific places, most of them on the Other Side. And many children, psychically sensitive as they are, happen to be tuned in to those stations from which the information is being transmitted.

A child has many, many ways of uncovering information about the present and future, which we'll discuss in detail in Chapter Seven. As you'll see, there's no such thing as impossible or out of nowhere when that information turns out to be accurate. Even when it's only accurate a high percentage of the time it's worth paying attention to. Remember, no psychic child or adult on earth has a 100 percent accuracy rate. Only God has title to that claim.

I do want to emphasize one caution about children's dreams in which they seem to have been given either currently relevant knowledge or predictions for the future. These last two categories of dreams can easily be confused with release dreams. If, for example, a child tells you they dreamed of a family member dying, do not leap to the conclusion that it's prophetic and fly into a panic. There's an equally good chance they're simply expressing through a release dream their fear of losing someone they love. The only hard and fast rule for telling the difference is the eventual discovery of whether or not the information turned out to be accurate. Mind you, if that dream involved a detail like, let's say, a car accident in a blue truck, or a fall down a long flight of stairs, I might avoid hopping into a blue truck for a while, and/or be especially careful when descending long flights of stairs. But that's only because I'm a big believer in erring on the side of caution whenever possible.

And just one more footnote: For those of you who've come to the conclusion that your children aren't psychic after all because they don't seem to have prophetic dreams, I want you to know that even with the wealth of psychic gifts I've been given, not once in my life—not even as a child—have I ever had a dream that accurately predicted the future. Just as with God-given gifts in every other area of life on earth, the specifics vary from one child to the next, but they're all equally valuable in His eyes.

Astral Catalepsy

"A few times a month," wrote Elise, "my four-year-old daughter, Millie, wakes up screaming in the middle of the night. I race into her room and she tells me that a monster, or sometimes a 'bad man,' woke her up, making horrible growling noises. It, or he, climbed on top of her and wouldn't let her move or breathe or make a sound. Even though she doesn't know the words to say, from what she

177

describes it almost sounds as if whatever this evil presence is tried to molest her. By the time she's able to cry out, the monster is gone, so my searching the room to prove to her that no one's there and everything's fine doesn't comfort her very much. I don't understand what's going on and why my child is being terrorized like this. (I'd be lying if I said I'm not as terrorized as she is when it happens.) She has nightmares every once in a while, but they don't compare to this. Is this some extreme form of nightmare, or is something evil targeting her for some reason? And whatever it is, what can I do to help my daughter?"

I have hundreds if not thousands of similar letters in my files, so I won't be surprised if your child has experienced some equally terrifying version of what that child is going through. And if that's the case, I want to assure you of two things right up front: It's not a nightmare, and *there's very definitely nothing evil attacking your child while he or she sleeps.*

Instead, your child is being involuntarily subjected to a common, mystifying, and fascinating phenomenon called astral catalepsy. It's not a disease, and it's not an affliction your child necessarily has to look forward to for life, although many adults suffer from it as well. It's a temporary physiological reaction—and an ultimately harmless one, even though it couldn't feel more threatening—to a few moments when the spirit and the body are, for lack of a better description, out of synch. And its symptoms typically include any or all of the following:

* a sensation of paralysis
* struggling to breathe, from the feeling of an oppressive weight on the chest
* an inability to cry out, or even make a sound

✳   being touched in an obscene or malicious way by an invisible presence

✳   a pervasive vibration, either from deep within the body or surrounding it

✳   being pinned down and immobilized by some unseen evil

✳   a clamor of noises, from a buzz to an electronic-sounding hum to a roaring wind to a chaotic blare as if a room full of fifty different TV channels are turned on to full volume all at the same time

✳   flashes of strange, glaring lights

✳   a sincere, terrifying belief that a vicious entity of some kind is either sitting on the edge of the bed or is deliberately disturbing the bedding

All that, from something as routine and as natural to us as breathing.

We've already discussed the fact that several times a week, children's spirits take off from their bodies while they sleep, to visit loved ones, to explore, to reunite with past lives, to enjoy the blissful comfort of Home and to simply escape the limiting confines of earth. These spirit trips, or astral travels, are nourishing, refreshing escapes that keep children connected to the spirit world of the Other Side and to their own eternal God-centered spirit selves.

The vast majority of the time, children's spirits come and go from their bodies with the greatest of ease, while their conscious minds go right on sleeping, undisturbed and unaware. But on rare occasions, especially if the conscious mind is making a transition from one level or depth of sleep to another, it can suddenly catch the spirit leaving or entering the body. And there's only one obvious conclusion the earthly conscious mind leaps to on discovering that the spirit is only half in or half out: The body must be dying. It panics and sends emergency alerts to the body that it's dying, and the body instantly reacts in appropriate ways that correspond to many of the sensations in the list of astral catalepsy symptoms: the paralysis, the inability to breathe or cry out, the fear, and the physiological and neurological certainty that something terrible is happening and death is imminent.

It's also important to remember that the spirit world from which children come and go when they astrally travel is a different dimension and a much higher frequency level than they're living in here on earth. Astral travel by definition involves the transition from one dimension to another. The assault of noises and lights that the conscious mind picks up as the spirit returns to the body is not unlike the phenomenon of a sonic boom, the audible shock wave that happens when supersonic aircraft reenter the earth's atmosphere. The sudden, unpleasant sensation of being pinned down by some unseen oppressive heaviness is the conscious mind being momentarily aware of the spirit's traveling from the weightlessness of the spirit world to the gravity of earth.

Add all those sensations together and it's an overwhelming, insanely confusing and literally shocking assault for the semisleeping conscious mind to deal with all at once. But the instant the conscious mind registers that the spirit has returned safe and sound to the body again, it sends the appropriate signals that death isn't imminent after all and, in fact, everything seems to be back to normal again. And on those signals, the symptoms of astral catalepsy stop and the child is left with no real harm to recover from, other than a chaotic few moments of terror.

In case you think your child has been singled out to suffer through occasional struggles with astral catalepsy, or that it's some relatively new affliction, please know, and share with your child, that it's been scaring children, and grown-ups—without a single injury or incident of genuine danger—for thousands of years. Cultures around the world have been fascinated and mystified by it for so long that they've created some amazingly colorful folklore to try to explain what goes on during a typical astral catalepsy episode.

Northern European folklore theorized that astral catalepsy, or sleep paralysis, as it's sometimes called, was caused by witches who abducted unwitting sleepers and took them for long broomstick rides to distant, mystical places. The Japanese devised a scenario they named *kanashibari,* in which a gigantic devil would sneak into bedrooms during the night and pin sleeping people to their beds with its foot. Newfoundland came up with the legend of the Old Hag, a hideous witch who would sit on sleepers' chests and wrap her gnarled, claw-like hands around their necks in an effort to strangle them. China called it *gui ya,* to describe a ghost who, they theorized, was sitting on sleeping people and assaulting them, and the West Indians arrived at a variation on gui ya that they called *kokma,* which was actually a baby ghost, jumping up and down on sleeping people's chests. And many ardent UFO believers have decided that astral catalepsy is obviously caused by aliens who abduct sleeping humans while they're at their most vulnerable and take that opportunity to perform examinations and experiments on them.

The actual term astral *catalepsy* wasn't coined until around 1930, by a researcher named Sylvan Muldoon. He spent much of his life recording the astral trips his spirit took at night while his body slept. The first astral trip he was aware of happened when he was twelve years old, and it inspired his intensive exploration of what he'd only heard referred to until then as sleep paralysis.

It started with his waking up in the middle of the night to find himself unable to move, see, or hear, with a painful sense of severe pressure on his head. As his senses and ability to move slowly returned, and the pressure on his head subsided, he realized that he was actually outside his body, floating above his bed and able to look down and watch himself sleep. He was aware of his spirit being pulled from a horizontal position to a vertical one as it left his body, and in that vertical position he, in spirit form, embarked on a tour of the house, during which he was able to move with great ease through doors and walls. He made a conscious effort to enter his parents' bedroom and try to shake them awake because he was so frightened of what was happening to him, but they never seemed to feel him touching them.

When he was finally above his body again, his spirit eased back into a horizontal position, and he experienced the same paralysis, loss of senses, and pressure on his head that he'd gone through when the astral trip began. After a feeling of being jerked abruptly back into his body, he sat bolt upright in bed in a complete panic.

Fortunately for all of us, Sylvan Muldoon had total recall of everything that happened to him before, during, and after his sleep paralysis, and he immediately wrote down the whole sequence of events. It put the sleep paralysis, which he renamed astral catalepsy, into the context of being the beginning and end of an astral excursion, that moment when the spirit leaves the body and that moment when it returns. It became a recurring experience throughout his life and the subject of some of his most exhaustive research, and it's thanks to him and countless other researchers he inspired that you can explain to your child what causes their occasional astral catalepsy and, above all, that there's never a moment during it when they're not perfectly safe.

I wish I could promise that if you follow the suggestions I'm about to offer, your child will never, ever experience astral catalepsy again, but I won't make promises I can't keep. What I can promise is that, at the very least, they'll help.

First, make a habit of talking to God with your child before they fall asleep. As you talk, I want you to surround your child with the all-loving, all-protecting white light of the Holy Spirit, and mix that divine light with swirls of rich, healing green. Then add the following to your prayers, in either my words or your own:

> Dear Father, if my child's spirit should travel tonight during sleep, please help their spirit exit and reenter their body with the divine, peaceful ease You taught them, with no awareness or interference from their easily frightened conscious mind.

Include that in your prayers every night, and teach it to your child. And then, if they should find themselves in the throes of astral catalepsy anyway, teach your child to pray again the instant they feel it coming over them. Teach them to surround themselves with the white light of the Holy Spirit, with healing green light swirling through it. Children are brilliant at visualizing, and all they need is your guidance to be bathed in the glow of God's love. Teach them to ask for His protection, and the divine protection of their Angels, and to keep right on praying until those scary sensations have passed, as you can safely promise they will. Prayers won't summon God and the Angels to your child's rescue; they'll just help remind your child that their most sacred protectors are already and eternally there.

Nightmares and Night Terrors

"My daughter Emily has seen spirits and ghosts all her life," wrote Barbara. "She was always okay with it until she started preschool at the age of four, at a house where she said there was a 'big man ghost with a black coat' who kept staring at her. Next thing I knew she was having nightmares where the ghost from preschool was chasing her with a big knife, and she would run all the way home to her room with him right behind her and when she hid from him under her bed he would assault her and try to choke her. She's had this dream so often that I'm starting to wonder if it is a dream or if maybe this ghost really is tracking her down and attacking her during the night, although she never has any marks or injuries in the morning."

Ken wrote, "My son Kevin started having night terrors when he was four years old. He never could tell me what caused them or what they were about, but he would wake up hysterical with fear and it could take up to a few hours to calm him down. That lasted until he was almost six, and then he could remember what scared him so much in his sleep. A lot of times there was a monster with spikey hair and huge red eyes, chasing him through a place where he was surrounded by boulders. Kevin would find a place to hide between the boulders and always wake up just as the monster found him. A few times he was running and hiding from something in our house that he couldn't see, but he knew it wanted to kill him or our family. I can comfort him and calm him down when he wakes up in such a panic, but I'm sure it would be more helpful to him if I could explain why he keeps going through this. The thing is, though, I can't explain it if I don't understand it myself."

I chose those two letters out of huge piles of virtually identical ones because they bring up several points I want to make, in no particular order, about nightmares and night terrors:

Never, ever believe, or perpetuate the belief to your child, that spirits or ghosts can or would harm them. They can't and won't attack them or assault them or perform lewd acts on them or violate them in any way. If your child thinks such a thing happened, I guarantee you with my hand to God that what they really experienced was either a nightmare or some form of the astral catalepsy we discussed in the previous section. (And this is true for adults as well, by the way. It simply never happens. Period.)

The vast majority of children's nightmares, almost without exception, involve being chased. It's a combination of jumbled frightening moments from past lifetimes and the growing awareness of frightening elements in this new lifetime. Studies have shown that children don't start having nightmares until the age of three. At that age their past lives are still very real to them, while at the same time they've had time to be exposed to tension, anxiety, and potential danger in the lifetime they're just beginning, none of which they were accustomed to in their lives on the Other Side. Never forget or underestimate how psychically sensitive children are. They'll pick up anger, resentment, stress, and unhappiness around them without even trying, no matter how well everyone thinks they're disguising or suppressing it. And since negative emotions are still alien to very young children, they have no context in which to put them and no way of knowing what might or might not escalate to a real, serious threat. The same goes for unedited television and movies, and for the more hideous of common fairy tales and lullabies—without context and a sense of discernment, psychically sensitive children can't reasonably be expected to separate fact from fiction, especially when they're still trying to adjust to their newly blended realities of the spirit world and the earthly world.

When my children and grandchildren were very young, I never let them anywhere near anything but the most child-oriented television shows, absolutely nothing violent or scary, no monsters or aliens, and nothing that would even imply that it's acceptable to be cruel or to hurt anyone. I also refused to tell them stories, no matter how classic, about witches who cooked children and ate them, or giants at the top of beanstalks who chased frightened little boys, or evil queens with poison apples, or bears chasing little girls who'd wandered into their house and fallen asleep, or babies falling out of trees in their cradles "when the bough breaks." I never even hinted that there might be such a thing as a boogeyman, or a monster under their bed, or some horrible ogre of some kind hiding in their closet, and I certainly never sang them to sleep with songs in which babies and their cradles fell out of trees, or taught them prayers that included the possibility that they might die before they woke. And I swear to you, not one child that was raised in my house ever suffered from nightmares or night terrors. Not one.

Monsters by any name and description that appear in a child's dreams are always nothing more and nothing less than a physical embodiment of fears, insecurities, anger, frustration, confusion, loneliness, and other negative emotions they're experiencing while they're awake and don't know how to express. They (and we) naturally create actual evil creatures while we sleep for the simple, obvious reason that negativity feels more manageable and less overwhelming if we have something tangible to point to that we can theoretically touch, feel, and, ideally, defeat.

And a little food for thought that will always mystify me: How many parents do you know who wouldn't dream (pardon the expression) of teaching their children about the marvelous inhabitants of the spirit world who come to visit them and sometimes fill their rooms at night, but are perfectly comfortable filling their heads with stories of boogeymen and ogres and other vicious creatures who just might leap out at them from the shadows, snatch them, and eat them alive if they don't behave? Spirits and ghosts are ridiculous fantasies, but monsters aren't? Is that a worthwhile, God-centered message to pass along to a child?

The only real difference between nightmares and night terrors is that children can usually remember their nightmares, but they invariably remember nothing about the cause of their night terrors. It's as if their conscious minds have no intention of addressing whatever frightened them so much while they slept, so they simply block it out. While that makes night terrors very difficult to analyze and explore, I'm convinced that a major percentage of night terrors are caused by episodes of astral catalepsy. I'm basing some of that belief on the fact that when I was a child, I often suffered from night terrors myself. I don't remember any more about what caused them than other children do. But I have a confession to make: I frankly don't enjoy astral travel. It's happened to me a few times while I was meditating and practicing yoga. For a second or two I kind of got a kick out of the novelty of looking down at my own body from somewhere near the ceiling, but I very quickly became aware of feeling not in control and didn't like it. Bearing that in mind, I can easily imagine that waking up as a child to find that my spirit was just coming home from its travels might have upset me more than enough to trigger a night terror. And I'm sure that my mother, who believed that stories of boogeymen in the closet and monsters under the bed were efficient ways of keeping me from getting up during the night and disturbing her sleep, made her share of contributions to my night terrors as well.

I discussed this in a previous chapter, but I want to remind you of it here as well. And I'll also repeat that I don't care if you believe it will help your child or not—just do it. Every night, ideally from the moment you bring your new baby home right on through their early grade school years, make a habit of sitting beside their bed when you know they're asleep. Surround them with the white light of the Holy Spirit. And then, very quietly, so you don't wake them up, give them the following affirmation:

> Precious child, tonight as you sleep, wherever your dreams and journeys take you, let all the fear and pain and illness and negativity you brought with you from your past lives be released and resolved forever into the cleansing white light of the Holy Spirit that surrounds you now. Let all the joy and love from those past lives infuse you and bless you in this new lifetime you've chosen to share with me. May your spirit travel safely without disturbing you, and may it return to bring you peace, comfort, and the bliss of God's perfect love as you sleep soundly in His arms.

There's also a valuable technique you can teach your child to make their nightmares less traumatic and remind them of their personal power at the same time. And while you're at it, you might want to work on this technique yourself. I conducted a series of dream seminars for many years, and it was fascinating for everyone involved to discover that a) this technique, relatively simple as it is, rarely occurs to us as a possibility, and b) it can transform even the most upsetting nightmare (and release dream, for that matter) into a victory.

The technique is as simple as this: Program your child to remember that with practice, they can rewrite the ending to any dream they want. They can create their own happy ending if a dream begins to make them too frightened or sad. When they tell you they dreamed of being chased by a monster, be sympathetic and comfort them, but then suggest that the next time it happens, they can just turn around, look that monster right in the eye, and yell at it to go away, and it will. When they tell you they dreamed they woke up and found themselves all alone in the house as if the rest of the family moved away and abandoned them, suggest that the next time it happens, all they have to do is open one more door as they search and they'll find the whole family right there waiting for them, because they would never, ever leave them behind. Whatever the nightmare or release dream, help them devise a way to continue the story in such a way that they come out on top in the end. Again, it is a way for them to exercise some of their power while they sleep, so simple and obvious but an option that occurs to us so rarely. It won't completely eliminate bad dreams, nor do we want to—as we discussed in the section on release dreams, it's healthy for children, and for us, to let off some steam during sleep. But it will help, I promise you that.

Participating in Your Child's Dreams

There are a lot of well-intentioned parents who, for one reason or another, don't ask their child more than a few passing questions at best about their dreams. Some of them are afraid to seem too eager about it, not wanting to imply that they'll be disappointed if the child can't remember or if the dream wasn't all that interesting. Others avoid the subject for fear that if the child's dreams are troubling, they won't have a clue what to say or do to help. Some aren't convinced that there's much importance in dreams to begin with. And, sadly, still others simply don't take the time to have the conversation.

If any of those descriptions apply to you, please just ask yourself if it would have been helpful if, when you were a child, someone had taught you how to understand and make friends with your dreams. Wouldn't it have been a relief to know that your release dreams weren't real; they were just your way of letting off steam during the night? Wouldn't you love to have learned that turning around and squaring off with the monsters that chased you was a healthy, empowering option? Wouldn't you have appreciated hearing about the wonderful people and places and times you can astrally visit without fear while you sleep, and about the ultimately harmless astral catalepsy that might happen every once in a while as your spirit comes and goes from your body? Wouldn't it have added to your confidence while you slept to know that whatever happened, you'd be able to make sense of it when you woke up, rather than feeling like a sitting duck for any images and stories and information that might come springing out at you for no good reason? Wouldn't you have felt more at peace with yourself to have been assured that when you woke up knowing something you didn't know when you went to sleep the night before, either about the present or the future, there would be explanations for where that knowing came from, and that it didn't mean you weren't normal?

There's not a doubt in my mind that you answered yes to at least one of those questions. It's for that reason that I can't urge you enough to stop and think what a difference you could make to a child for the rest of their life by developing the habit of regular conversations that start with the simple, invaluable words, "Tell me about your dreams."

And then, if you really want to enhance the dream experience for your child, and give yourself an education beyond your wildest expectations, take an extra five minutes out of your day after those conversations and start keeping a dream journal on your child's behalf until they're old enough to do it on their own. Sit down and read it with them every few months. They'll appreciate looking back on the scary dreams they've survived, the wonderful people and places they've visited but might have forgotten, the information they've picked up along the way that turned out to be true, the fears they expressed in release dreams that by now have worked themselves out, and the wish dreams they no longer remember that might have come true or that they no longer care about. Above all, they'll appreciate that their dreams were important enough—and therefore so were they—that you took the time to pay attention and write them down. Can you think of a more magical gift to give them, that won't cost you a dime? Neither can I.

CHAPTER SEVEN

Kinetic Children

My son Paul had just turned thirteen, which is to say he'd just entered the wonderful world of puberty. We had dinner one evening as usual, he did his homework as usual, and then he headed off to his room to go to bed, closing his door behind him as usual. What wasn't usual at all was that several minutes later I heard a loud, seemingly endless barrage of thuds coming from inside Paul's room. It honestly sounded as if my son had put on his heaviest pair of work boots and was tap dancing all over the floor, walls, and ceiling. I rushed to his room and carefully opened the door, not one bit sure what I was stepping into. I might have been less surprised to find him tap dancing on the ceiling in his work boots. Paul was sound asleep in bed. And all around him, every shoe he owned was careening wildly around the room, bouncing off the walls, size 10 jet-propelled leather and canvas rockets with no one at the controls. I was at a complete loss about what to do, so after ducking to avoid a flying high-top sneaker, I impulsively yelled, "Paul! Stop that!" He stirred a little in bed, woke up for a second or two, and went right back to sleep again. During those brief moments, all his shoes dropped to the floor and stayed there where they belonged for the rest of the night.

From that night on for many, many months, at least three or four nights a week, I'd suddenly hear Paul's shoes rocketing around his room after he went to bed. I didn't bother to go in again, I just yelled, "Paul! Stop that!" from outside his door and within seconds the noises would stop.

This same kind of thing may have gone on in your house, or you still may have it to look forward to if you have a child in the house. Cupboards and drawers may start flying open and slamming shut, appliances may spring to life all by themselves, lights may begin blinking wildly, your TV may go racing uncontrollably from one channel to another on its own, computers may crash, phones may suddenly offer nothing but static, all triggered by nothing more than your child strolling into the room. And you don't necessarily have until they hit puberty to brace yourself. As I told you in Chapter Two, my granddaughter Angelia was only five or six years old when we realized we couldn't let her near any electrical appliance or piece of office equipment without running the risk of malfunctions, short circuits, complete breakdowns, and even a burned wire or two.

You have my word that, should you find yourself on the receiving end of this chaos, you're not alone. And while some of the above can be caused by ornery ghosts, or spirits trying to get your attention, if you can reliably make a connection between the chaos and your child's presence, it's safe to assume that your child has the gift (although some would call it a curse) of kinetic energy.

Kinetic energy, also known in the paranormal world as psychokinesis or telekinesis, is the ability to move or manipulate inanimate objects without the use of any physical means. In the world of physics, *kinetic energy* is defined as "the energy of movement." *Telekinesis* is adapted from the Greek and, literally translated, means "distant movement." Psychokinesis combines the Greek words *psyche,* which means "life force" or "soul," and *kinein,* which means "to move." I prefer to simplify and demystify whenever possible, so I'll refer to the whole phenomenon as kinetic energy and trust you to understand.

Essentially, children who possess the power of kinetic energy can be thought of as walking force fields, or maybe human remote controls. Of the thousands of children I've met with kinetic energy, including the two in my family, I've never met a single one who deliberately used it to be disruptive or destructive. They're invariably as shocked as the rest of us at the insane behavior of the inanimate objects they trigger. And please don't be confused by the story of my son Paul and his flying shoes, and the fact that my yelling "stop that!" caused the episodes to end. Paul's kinetic energy seemed to take effect when he was asleep. My stopping it by yelling only worked because it momentarily woke him up. In fact, I feel safe in saying that while Angelia was kind of amused by the effects of her kinetic energy when she was a little girl, Paul wanted no part of it at age thirteen and was more relieved than anyone when it finally faded away.

I've read more studies, experiments, and research about kinetic energy than I can begin to count, and I feel safe in summarizing all of them by saying that there are almost as many theories about what causes it as there are experts who have explored it. And let's not forget the legions of skeptics who don't believe any such thing exists at all. I would happily have invited any of them to pay the repair bills on my office equipment after an innocent visit from Angelia, or to put Paul's countless pairs of shoes back in his closet, after one of these theoretically imaginary events.

Some researchers believe that kinetic energy can simply manifest itself in a child or adult out of nowhere and then disappear again just as inexplicably. Others believe, and I agree, that it's a specific energy force that some are born with and others aren't, and it tends to ebb and flow in usually unpredictable cycles throughout the course of a lifetime. Angelia's seems to have almost vanished since she was about six years old, while Paul never experienced it as a child but was hit with it full force when puberty came along, after which it was gone again. There does seem to be some connection between kinetic energy and dramatic hormonal changes, during puberty, pregnancy, and menopause, for example, and between kinetic energy and heightened emotions like fear or anger. But even then there's still no way of predicting whether it will or won't be triggered into action, let alone for how long. And there seems to be general agreement that it's not an inherited gift, which definitely holds true in my family—Paul and Angelia are the only two members of my family in three generations at the very least who were born with kinetic energy.

One of the more logical explanations I've read about how kinetic energy works goes as follows: Each of us has, as our essence, a divine spirit with its own energy, a spiritual life force the Chinese call *Chi* ("chee"). Our spirits in their natural state exist, as we know, in a world with a much higher frequency level than ours on earth. When kinetic energy affects inanimate objects in its path, it's because of a very specific effect of higher-frequency energy, combined with the earthly body's own physical energy, on solid matter that only exists in earth's lower frequency level. Oversimplified, it's the visible result of what happens when the infinite (spiritual energy) meets the finite (solid matter on earth).

But whatever its cause, and however often it occurs in the course of a lifetime, the fact remains that I've never met a child who deliberately manifested kinetic energy, or for whom it lasted for any significant length of time. But I have met far too many children whose involuntary kinetic energy has been misinterpreted as some vague physical or mental illness for which they were unnecessarily and often excessively medicated. And I've met far too many more whose innate, undisciplined kinetic energy has been mistaken for the child being possessed by evil, a subject that frankly makes my hair stand on end, not because the subject of possession frightens me but because *it doesn't exist.*

One of the most highly publicized cases of kinetic energy mistaken for demonic possession occurred in Pennsylvania in the early 1980s. The Rainboy Case, as it came to be known, involved a young man named Don Decker. By all accounts the bizarre series of events that unfolded around him were triggered when he attended the funeral of his grandfather. Don's grandfather was generally beloved among his family and friends. Don, on the other hand, remembered his grandfather as a man who had physically abused him, starting when he was seven years old, a secret he'd kept to himself and agonized over for years. The praise heaped upon Don's grandfather at the funeral and subsequent gathering at Don's family's home became too much for him to take, and he escaped to a friend's house to spend the night and regroup.

The rain began while Don was sitting in his friend's living room. Water began streaming down the walls, then pouring from the ceiling and seeping up through the floor, accompanied by a thick, swirling mist. Don's friend called his landlord, assuming a serious

197

plumbing problem had just sprung up. The landlord was both shocked and mystified by the incomprehensible room full of rain he walked in on, and he decided against calling a plumber for a very logical reason: The inexplicable water and mist were isolated to the room in the front half of the house where Don was sitting, but the only plumbing in the house was in the back half, where there were no problems at all. Calling a plumber to repair leaks in pipes that didn't exist seemed pointless.

The more the rain in the room continued, the more frightened and helpless Don, his friend, his friend's wife, and the landlord became, and finally, not knowing what else to do, they called the police.

The police were understandably skeptical at first, but it didn't take long for them to realize that whatever was going on, it was real, it was dramatic, and it was inexplicable. They'd never seen anything like it, particularly when they noticed that some of the streams of water weren't running straight down the wall like normal water; they were actually moving horizontally across the wall. While they inspected this unprecedented situation and tried to figure out what to do, they gave Don and his friends, who by now hadn't eaten or slept in far too many hours, permission to go to a small restaurant across the street for a quick bite to eat.

The instant Don left the house, the rain and mist vanished. And the instant he entered the restaurant, the same rain and mist started there. A waitress at the restaurant leapt to the only supposedly obvious conclusion she could come up with: Don was clearly possessed, possibly by the insidiously evil spirit of his grandfather, and the only possible remedy was an exorcism. As proof, she took a crucifix from around her neck and put it in his hand, where it reportedly burned him on contact.

Don and his friends returned to the house, triggering the rain and mist to start inside the home again. Desperate with fear, confusion, and frustration, his friends began lashing out at him, accusing him of deliberately causing all this chaos, upon which the electricity began flickering on and off, pots and pans in the kitchen began shaking and rattling insanely, and Don, with no one near him, was suddenly picked up by some invisible force and thrown across the room into a wall. The police and the landlord were still there and witnessed the whole bizarre sequence of events, but of course there was nothing they could do to help, and nothing they could even make sense of, so they left. The chief of police, who'd been summoned out of bed to the scene, was so shaken as he left that he ordered his officers not to write a report, to essentially forget those several hours ever happened.

The only member of the local clergy who was willing to attempt an exorcism was an evangelical minister. The effect was dramatic and purely temporary.

Before long Don landed in a maximum-security prison. None of the reports I've seen and read incidate the reason for his incarceration, but they consistently agree that it was completely unrelated to this strange phenomenon he was experiencing. And shortly after he arrived in prison, to the astonishment of everyone who saw it, it began to rain inside his cell, with the same swirling mist and water inexplicably pouring from the walls and ceiling and seeping up through the floor. Don now claimed to a prison worker that he himself was making it rain, by his own power and will, and if he chose to he could even make it rain in the warden's office. Minutes later that same worker stopped by the warden's office and, in shock, pointed out to an equally shocked warden that the front of the warden's shirt was drenched for no apparent reason.

The warden, assuming that whatever was going on was rooted in evil, called in the prison chaplain. The chaplain met privately with Don, who repeated his claim that he was the sole, deliberate cause of all the chaotic phenomena the chaplain was there to address. The ominous rain and mist swirled around them as if on cue, and the chaplain was suddenly overwhelmed by a thick, sickening odor that reminded him of the smell of death.

Deeply frightened in what he felt was the presence of the devil, the chaplain opened his Bible and began to read, aloud and intensely. He kept his wits about him enough to notice that while he read and the rain kept drenching him and Don, the pages of the Bible remained perfectly dry.

Then, as the chaplain continued to read, the rain and the mist stopped, as instantly as it had started. The repulsive odor vanished. And Don, possibly for the first time since what he considered to be the cruel hypocrisy of his grandfather's funeral, became utterly and completely peaceful.

Never again, after those hours with the chaplain, did Don Decker make it rain.

I want to clarify that I never met Don Decker, and my staff and I have been unsuccessful in trying to find any updates on him. I might be skeptical of the whole story if it weren't for the fact that at least eight or nine credible, objective witnesses, including police officers and prison officials who would rather not have seen a thing, verified the extraordinary events as they unfolded.

Assuming that even some of the events are true, it's a dramatic, fascinating story, and I also find it so sad. This young man was clearly in serious emotional distress as a direct result of the funeral of his grandfather, and that distress clearly triggered a frightening onslaught of incidents, every one of which was a powerful display of kinetic energy.

Strong kinetic energy in anyone, especially when it's unexpected and uncontrolled, can turn them into a kind of walking electrical force field. That force field can absolutely disrupt everything in its path, and it can certainly cause enough condensation to create rain and a swirling mist from humidity in the atmosphere or even any water pipes in the vicinity. When the force field goes away—i.e., when Don Decker left the house—the condensation stops, and as long as the power surge continues, that condensation will follow, as it followed Don Decker to the restaurant and eventually into a jail cell. Place any metal—like, in this case, a silver crucifix—onto what amounts to a live human electrical wire and you can count on it to get hot. Let that force field turn in on itself—like, in this case, when Don was being yelled at and accused of deliberately causing all the chaos—it can throw itself across the room, just like any strong jolt of electricity can send someone flying into a nearby wall. And if kinetic energy is powerful enough to dramatically affect water molecules, it can have the same effect on any ozone in the air, which is a key element of smog and, when mixed with other gases, can produce the awful odor of formaldehyde, much like the prison chaplain smelled in Don's presence.

If Don Decker finally became conscious enough of the power of the kinetic energy he was emitting, whether he really understood what it was or not, to the point where he could actually control it to some extent and focus it on the warden's office or anywhere else he chose, it's not surprising. I'm sure it was a case of accepting an undeniable affliction and doing his best to embrace it rather than continue his futile attempts to fight it.

The tragedy of this case to me is the thought of this disturbed, confused young man, who was victimized more than anyone else by the kinetic phenomena going on around him, being further victimized by fairly unanimous, terrorizing pronouncements that he was possessed by evil or by satan himself. Can you imagine anything more diminishing and discouraging when you're at the lowest, most mystifying, most dramatically out of control moments of your life than to be told that on top of everything else you're going through, the devil is now in charge of you?

You might argue that the exorcisms seemed to work. And in a way, they did, but not because actual exorcisms took place. Prayers and scripture readings didn't drive the devil away. *There is no devil.* They simply calmed him enough, and summoned his protectors from the Other Side effectively enough, that the kinetically charged phenomena around him subsided.

If and when I ever have a talk with Don Decker, you can be sure I'll spend as much time as it takes assuring him what I'm determined to assure you as well: I don't care how obvious the conclusion might seem in any given situation that evil has displaced God and a satanic possession has taken place. There's always some other explanation for that particular conclusion, because no other spirit than yours ever can or ever will possess your body.

And there are lessons for every family member of a kinetic child in the Don Decker story. For one thing, never underestimate the potential power of kinetic energy and the many ways it can manifest itself. For another thing, remember that no child asks to be born with the gift/burden of kinetic energy, and the manifestations of that energy can be just as startling, confusing, and frightening to the child as they are to you. For any kinetic child to essentially be punished for something over which they have no control, let alone accused of being evil or possessed because the adults around them simply don't understand the phenomenon of kinetic energy, is nothing short of heartbreaking.

The Truth About Demonic Possession

The paranormal definition of possession is that a foreign, usually evil spirit invades and completely overtakes the physical body without warning or consent, to the total submission of the spirit that's already inhabiting that body. In its most widely reported tabloid form, and in popular fiction both in print and on movie screens, the invading spirit is the very personification of evil and can only be defeated by being driven from the body by an ordained member of the clergy performing a highly dramatic exorcism.

I know there are many cultures and religions that believe in the possibility of demonic possession and the necessity of exorcisms, and I mean them no disrespect. But the truth is, the physical body being involuntarily overtaken by any other spirit than its own is a physiological, spiritual, and psychic impossibility. It can't be done.

As I keep saying throughout this book, think. God created a perfect, orderly, logical universe. We, His cherished children, are part of that universe. But what could be more imperfect, haphazard, and illogical than the possibility that every once in a while, at its own whim and convenience, some evil presence could simply displace our sacred spirits from our bodies and take up residence? A god who's either flawed, sloppy, or downright mean might have left room for something so perverse, but that's the very antithesis of the God we know, who gave us life and promised us unconditional, eternal love.

Over countless millennia humans, who are the only real source of evil in this world, have used the imaginary concept of possession and the cure of exorcism as kind of a handy catch-all excuse for abusing, neglecting, and manipulating children. It's been misused as a substitute for much-needed psychiatric and medical care. It's been threatened as punishment for disobedience or even just normal childhood behavior. It's been a quick, easy way of controlling children through fear and the destruction of their self-confidence— there are few more devastating things you can say to an adult, let alone a child, than, "You've been possessed by the devil and you need an exorcism." It's impossible to imagine how many scam artists and cult leaders have used false diagnoses of possession and the urgent need for an exorcism as their own personal paths to money and power. And in the end, there's only one thing you can count on when it comes to the subjects of possession and exorcism: They're creations of human beings, having nothing to do with God, for the sole purpose of frightening people into obedience. They have no basis in reality. They never did, and they never will. So whatever God-given powers and gifts your child might have, especially if those gifts seem as bizarre as kinetic energy often does, please keep words like *possession* and *exorcism* and *evil* and *demons* and *devil* out of your vocabulary. Instead, educate yourself, and them, about what's really going on and never suggest to them for a moment that anyone but God is guiding them.

To clear up any confusion you might be having about those occasions when Francine temporarily takes over my body—that is most definitely not possession. It's called *channeling*. A channel, like me, for example, is someone who receives spirit communication by going into an altered state of consciousness, usually a meditation or trance, and allows the spirit to literally speak through them. It never happens without my awareness and permission, and at no time does Francine replace my spirit with hers. I simply withdraw, or step aside temporarily, and become her receiver or her public address system so that she can communicate directly through me without my having to act as her interpreter. Again, and most importantly, unless I give my permission, it can't and won't happen.

Children arrive on this earth with inherently God-centered spirits. It's up to us to nourish that essential part of them, rather than confusing them with constant threats and warnings of evil. Someone was kind enough to share a story that illustrates that point beautifully:

One evening an old Cherokee told his grandson about a battle that goes on inside people.

"My son," he said, "the battle is between two wolves inside us all. One is Evil. It is anger, envy, jealousy, sorrow, regret, greed, arrogance, self-pity, guilt, resentment, inferiority, lies, false pride, superiority, and ego.

"The other is Good. It is joy, peace, love, hope, serenity, humility, kindness, benevolence, empathy, generosity, truth, compassion, and faith."

The grandson thought about it for a minute and then asked his grandfather, "Which wolf wins?"

The old Cherokee simply replied, "The one you feed."

Kinetic Energy and Healing

So far I've made kinetic energy in children sound like nothing but a potential source of temporary insanity among the inanimate objects around you. But that's only part of the story. Kinetic energy/

telekinesis/psychokinesis is also responsible for making healings possible.

During the same period of her childhood when my granddaughter Angelia was involuntarily decimating all our phones and office equipment, I also witnessed a private little miracle she performed in my backyard. We're a family of animal lovers, so it didn't surprise me when, before I could stop her, she ran to a little wounded bird she found lying in the grass and gently held it in both her hands. What did surprise me—in fact, it amazed me—was when, after a few moments, that little bird flew away without a hint of whatever injury or illness left it helpless in my yard.

That was far from my first exposure to a healing, but it was certainly the first time I witnessed it coming from a child so young. And while I'll never claim to know this beyond all doubt, I've done enough research on the subject of healing and experienced it myself often enough to believe that there was a connection between the power of Angelia's kinetic energy at that time in her life and her power to lift a wounded bird from the grass and send it soaring off into the sky. It's the connection between the inherent energy of the conscious human mind and the sacred, eternal energy of the higher-frequency spirit mind, whose combined effect on earthly matter can be dramatic, as we've seen. The bodies of all living things are earthly matter. So if kinetic energy can send physical matter in shoe form careening around a room, or short circuit and otherwise disrupt all sorts of electrical equipment, doesn't it make all the sense in the world that it could have just as powerful an impact on the atoms, molecules, and cells of our bodies and, as a result, generate a healing?

I think (or hope) that every legitimate, credentialed, and experienced doctor on earth would agree, whether they want to or not, that prayer can affect physical healing and sometimes even work miracles. And what does prayer consist of other than the projection of energy from both our conscious minds and our divine spirit minds/life forces in whatever perfect ratio God devised to create a result—which is the definition of kinetic energy/psychokinesis/telekinesis.

That's purely our end of it, of course. The answers to our prayers are in God's hands. And never doubt that He always answers our prayers. It's just that sometimes He says no.

So if and when you see signs of kinetic energy in a child around you, in the various forms that energy can take, don't let it frighten you. Don't fall into the trap of assuming that if something seems dramatically confusing, it must be evil. Above all, don't ever diminish your child by projecting negative, mythical ideas of possession and the devil, which teaches them, among other things, the mistaken belief that there is something in this universe more powerful than God. You know, and your spirit knows, that that's simply not true.

Instead, what better time to gently teach your kinetically gifted child to channel that amazing force field into healing and prayer? Teach them for their sake, and for the sake of a world in which, when it's all said and done, every one of us is here to learn to overcome negativity, not to encourage it and help it grow.

Remember, act on and teach your child the message of that wonderful story about the two wolves inside us: The wolf that survives is the wolf we feed.

CHAPTER EIGHT

Psychic Children's Special Gifts

So now we know that every child is psychic, and we also know why every child is psychic. But psychic gifts vary from one child to the next, in a fascinating array of specialties. It's exactly the same as a child born athletically gifted, who might be a natural on the basketball court or football field but never quite gets the hang of skiing or golf; or a child born with great artistic talent who excels at watercolor and oil paintings without showing any particular flair at sculpture; or a musically gifted child who's a genius on the piano or as a composer but hopeless at stringed or wind instruments. Similarly, one psychic child might be brilliant at predictions without being especially clairvoyant (able to see beings and objects from other dimensions). Another might be able to hold a physical object and sense an uncanny amount of information about the object's owner, and yet have no skill at predicting the future. Our God-given talents are all valuable. The specific ways in which they do and don't manifest themselves are just part of what makes each of us, and most certainly each of our children, so magnificently unique.

The one question I'm asked most often about psychic children, once the parent has run across too many undeniable indications that their child is gifted, is, "How can I help them develop their psychic abilities?" And Chapter Ten will offer any number of exercises and suggestions on that subject. But before we even address the area of developing your children's psychic abilities, it's important to understand the many forms their psychic gifts might take, if for no other reason than to teach your children to understand them, appreciate them, and be proud of them as they would be with any of the other talents God gave them.

The Gift of Prophecy

Depending on your upbringing, culture, and religion, chances are that your mental stereotype of a prophet is either an ancient bearded man in robes or a woman in a turban and caftan hunched over a crystal ball. So when a child blurts out what reveals itself to be an accurate prediction of a future event—which is the definition of prophecy—it can be a shock, let's face it. It can also make you scramble to come up with any other ostensibly reasonable explanation, no matter how ridiculous, for how your child knew about something that hadn't happened yet with no apparent indications that it was going to happen. But once you've eliminated all the reasonable explanations, it's time to face the fact (and celebrate it) that your child, like countless other children, has the gift of prophecy.

(I'm suddenly reminded of a quotation from Sir Arthur Conan Doyle by way of his brilliant literary creation Sherlock Holmes. To paraphrase: "When every possibility has been exhausted, it's time to consider the impossible.")

Jolene's eight-year-old son, Ty, had chronically misunderstood behavioral problems at school—tragically, as sometimes happens, his teachers, counselors, psychologists, and principals believed that Ty's unapologetic discussions of seeing and hearing the spirit world translated to mental health problems and a need for antipsychotic medication. Jolene wasn't sure whether to believe her son's adamant claims about the rich visions and voices he'd experienced since he was an infant or the school's insistence that he was in serious psychological trouble. But a casual conversation with Ty one day convinced her to give him the strong benefit of the doubt. "Because of his disruptive behavior he spent more time with the principal and her secretary than most kids did, and he liked them both. One afternoon when I went to pick him up from school the principal told me that she and her secretary were both leaving for jobs at other schools. On the way home Ty said he was going to miss the principal. I said, 'What about her secretary? Aren't you going to miss her too?' He said, 'No. She'll be back.' There was such certainty in the way he said it that it took me aback, although I didn't say anything at a time. The end of the story is, the principal's job at the other school was and is a big success, but the secretary's new job fell through and she was back at my son's school a week later. I don't know how or why my son knew what was going to happen like that, but he did, and I'm not as quick to dismiss his visions and voices as I was before."

"We were on a family vacation," wrote Missy, "and my typically outgoing, happy, playful four-year-old child, Elena, started screaming when we pulled into a motel for the night. She kept saying the bad man in the black clothes with the black head might hurt us. She'd never talked like that before, and we took her seriously but we were too exhausted to drive on to another motel, so we checked in there and we were still trying to calm her down when we got to our room.

We went to bed, but a little while later my husband heard noises outside our room. He looked out the window and there was a man dressed in black, wearing a black ski mask, breaking into the snack machine with a crowbar. The motel clerk had already seen the man and called the police, and they caught the man before he could get away, or God forbid, use that same crowbar to break into someone's room, like maybe ours, and hurt someone or worse. There's no doubt about it, my daughter saw that coming hours before it happened."

"My son Cody has always seemed to be 'plugged in' to some world the rest of us can't perceive," wrote Wendy. "We've written a lot of it off to his extremely creative mind, but some things have become hard to dismiss. For example, on his fifth birthday I took him to a carnival in a town thirty miles from ours. We were on the way home when he suddenly yelled, 'Look out for the red truck on fire!' I had no idea what he was talking about and thought maybe he was still just keyed up from a day at the carnival. But about three or four miles later, around way too many curves for him to have seen it when he announced it, we came across a red truck on the shoulder of the highway with its engine engulfed in flames. I asked him how he knew that truck was on fire ahead of us and all he said was, 'I don't know, I just did.' "

Doug shared a similar story about his three-year-old son, Adrian. "We were driving across town for a visit with my parents to show them my son Adrian's new puppy. The traffic was pleasantly light for a change, so I couldn't have been more shocked when out of nowhere Adrian screamed, 'Daddy, stop, right now!' It's a good thing the traffic was light, because he startled me so much that I instinctively slammed on the brakes. For a split second I didn't see a thing that would have prompted him to scream like that. But another split second later one of those huge water delivery trucks came blasting

212

out of a blind alley to our left and blew past us into the alley to our right. It missed our front bumper by not even a foot. There's no way around it; if my son hadn't screamed, that truck would have broadsided us and probably killed us. I told Adrian it was a lucky thing he'd seen it coming and he said, 'I didn't see it with my real eyes; I saw it with my other eyes.' Whatever that means. And I'm not sure I even care. All I care about is that either his real eyes or his other eyes saved our lives that day."

"My daughter Ariana has been psychic since the day she was born," wrote Cheryl. "She would giggle and play with what I'm sure were visiting spirits above her when I put her in her crib for her nap, and ever since she was old enough to talk she was making comments to people about things she couldn't possibly know. When Ariana was five my best friend, Lorraine, came to visit for a few days. She and her husband wanted children very much, but she'd never been able to carry a child to full term, and they'd finally even given up on the fertility treatments they'd been trying for a couple of years. She told me all this on the phone before she got to our house but put on a happy face and didn't say a word about it once she arrived. The first morning Lorraine was there, she and Ariana and I did a grocery run. While we were in the store Ariana disappeared for a few minutes and then came running back up to us holding a balloon. She handed it to Lorraine and said, 'This is for you.' It was a pink balloon with the word 'It's A Girl!' written on it. It was kind of an awkward but innocent mistake. We thought. It turned out Lorraine was pregnant at the time without even knowing it, and eight and a half months later she gave birth to a beautiful, healthy baby girl."

That's just a tiny sampling of the letters and e-mails in my files from parents of children with the gift of accurately glimpsing the future. The tone of all this correspondence ranges from amazement to concern to disbelief to total confusion. Not surprising, since with no understanding of where the information comes from and how children retrieve it, the ability to predict the future can seem downright spooky. But once again, *think*. If a child has accurate knowledge of something that hasn't happened yet, it's simple logic, in God's logical universe, that a) that information has to already exist somewhere, and b) it has to get from somewhere into the child's consciousness in order for them to communicate it. And by unraveling the mysteries of those two statements of fact, we can easily make sense of this fascinating and very common gift.

Where Information About the Future Exists

The sources of all accurate predictions and prophecies physically exist on the Other Side. To understand that, there are some basic things you need to know about the Other Side itself.

In Chapter One we discussed that it's a very real place with a much higher frequency level than ours on earth, with its ground level only three feet above ours. Its landscape is almost identical to the topography of earth, with mountains and meadows and oceans and forests, all of the beauty of this planet untouched by the ravages of erosion and pollution and then magnified to a breathtaking magnificence that transcends our ability to capture it in words. My book *Life on the Other Side* is a thorough, detailed study of that world we all know as Home, so I'll only touch on a few relevant highlights here and encourage you to explore in depth in that book if you like and hope I'm not doing it an injustice in this discussion.

The architecture on the Other Side is as stunning as its varied landscape, particularly when it comes to the buildings that greet us on our arrival back Home. Each of these buildings at the entrance to the Other Side has its own specific purpose. The domed white marble Hall of Wisdom houses, among other things, the Scanning Machine, where we review the lives we've just left behind on earth. The Hall of Justice, a classic Greco-Roman monument surrounded by unspeakably beautiful Gardens, is the meeting place for the revered Council, also known as the Master Teachers. And completing the triumvirate of structures at its entrance is the vast, treasured Hall of Records.

The Hall of Records sits to the left of the Hall of Wisdom, its glittering dome towering above the surrounding hills and meadows. Among the infinite writings that line the endless, impeccably tended aisles of shelves in the Hall of Records lie the keys to predicting the future.

You've read about the detailed **life charts** we write before we come here for a new incarnation. Please take it literally that we *write* our charts, on parchment scrolls, and bear in mind that we write a chart for every incarnation we spend on earth. The vast majority of us have had dozens of incarnations, which translates to dozens of parchment scrolls for every human spirit currently living both here and on the Other Side. And every chart of every incarnation of every spirit ever born since time began is perfectly intact in perfect order in aisle after vast aisle of the Hall of Records.

Every life chart in the Hall of Records is accessible to every spirit on earth and at Home, with one exception: None of us is allowed to read our own chart for the lifetime we're currently living. We'll experience intuitions, coincidences, déjà vu, and countless other momentary indications that we remember the charts we wrote, but so that we can fully experience what we're here to accomplish, we're never given the opportunity to view what lies ahead in our own lives.

We can, though, study anyone and everyone else's charts we choose, as can everyone in the spirit world, including our Spirit Guides and our departed loved ones. And children, whose spirit lives on the Other Side are still more familiar to them than living on earth in a human body, are well aware of their access to those charts in the Hall of Records. It takes less than a heartbeat for a child's spirit, awake or asleep, to travel Home for a glimpse of a loved one's chart, whether they're consciously aware of the trip or not. The spirit world around them, with whom we know they regularly communicate, can also transmit past, present, and future information to them from those same charts, in ways we'll discuss momentarily.

Also kept in divine perfection in the Hall of Records on the Other Side are the **Akashic Records**, which are the other reliable source of predictions and all other knowledge among the spirit world. They've been described in several different ways by several different people and religions over the course of countless millennia. The brilliant "Sleeping Prophet" Edgar Cayce wrote of them as "the collective memories and histories of every thought, sound, vibration, moment, and event in eternity," while psychologist Carl Jung called them the Collective Unconscious, a conceptual entity of immeasurable power. The Hindus worshipped them as "every thought, word, and action," recorded on a sacred substance called *akasha,* which in their religion was the most basic and primary principle of nature, the substance from which earth, water, fire, and air were created.

My definition of the Akashic Records, shared by many other

scholars, researchers, and my Spirit Guide Francine, doesn't contradict any of these other descriptions; it's simply, for me, clearer and more tangible. The Akashic Records are the actual written memory of God. Their sacred power is undoubtedly imprinted on the very life force of the universe, but they also exist in the physical form of the Other Side, on countless sacrosanct scrolls in the Hall of Records. They're written in Aramaic, the language we all speak fluently at Home, and they're accessible to every spirit God ever created, including, of course, our children. And if you just flashed on the thought that your child is too young to read, you've momentarily forgotten that regardless of your child's current physical age, their spirit is as ancient as time itself, and the Akashic Records are more divinely familiar to them than any bedtime story you'll ever use to read them to sleep.

The infinite knowledge housed in the Hall of Records can't be communicated by a child until the child becomes aware of it, obviously. Past, present, or future; relatively trivial or of major significance; whether or not the child is conscious of how it came to them, all that information a child couldn't possibly know finds its way into their minds through a fascinating variety of methods. We all arrive perfectly adept at these methods. It's just that children haven't spent enough time on earth to become too sophisticated (read cynical) to embrace the wisdom and the worlds beyond our own.

We discussed **astral travel** at length in Chapter Six, so I won't belabor it again here. But one of the ways that children access the information in the Hall of Records is by simply going there themselves, awake or asleep, and looking it up. Again, like the rest of us, children aren't allowed a single glimpse at their own charts—it would be like cheating on a test, or reading ahead in a mystery novel for us to be able to read our charts. But they can certainly read anyone else's, and don't forget, the chart you wrote includes every detail of your life, even if it hasn't happened yet. In less than the blink of an eye they can skip ahead a moment, a week, a month, a year, whenever they want, and essentially read back to you what you yourself wrote. And from time to time, they might even have some conscious awareness of their quick astral trip. When, for example, a child makes a comment about seeing a future moment not with their "real eyes" but with their "other eyes," rest assured that those other eyes belong to their spirit, traveling Home to bring you some bit of news from your future that you need to know.

Don't forget another fascinating possibility about a child's glimpse into your future on those occasions when it actually seems to intervene in your chart: Since you and your child charted yourselves into each other's lives before you met again here on earth, it's likely that you also charted your child to intervene at exactly the right moment. There really is nothing haphazard about the ways our lives connect and affect each other, just as there's nothing haphazard anywhere else in God's creation.

It's not always necessary for a child to astrally travel to the Hall of Records on the Other Side to gather information from life charts and the Akashic Records. Spirit Guides and the rest of the spirit world have access to that same information, and they can easily pass it along to psychic children. Sometimes they do it audibly, in the high-pitched chirps of spirit voices traveling from their dimension to ours. At other times, though, they simply use the silent communication of **telepathy**.

Telepathy is the direct, instantaneous passing of information from one mind, or consciousness, to another without the use of the five physical senses of sight, hearing, touch, taste, or smell. In tele-pathic communication, a sender transmits information to a receiver, and it can happen deliberately or without either the sender or the receiver being aware of it.

Most information sent telepathically is meant to have some meaning to the receiver, and/or to be acted upon, so it's shared with the conscious mind in a variety of forms: words or phrases that pop into the mind for no apparent reason, quick flashes of half-complete images, or unusually clear dreams. When a child with the gift of pre-cognition receives information about the future and says it's some-thing they just heard, it's very possible that the information came to them through telepathy.

The spirit world in general is particularly adept at telepathy. Ask any child who's had an encounter with a deceased loved one, or most especially an Angel, and they'll often describe long, detailed conversations in which neither of them spoke a single word. (As we discussed in Chapter Five, Angels *never* speak. Their communica-tion with us and with each other is exclusively telepathic.) And if you have the joy of being close to an animal, by the way, you don't need me to tell you how much those divine spirits telepathically send if you'll simply take the time to tune in and receive. Telepathy is their most common form of communication with each other, after all, and they happen to be brilliant at it.

Telepathy isn't limited by time or distance, and it's also not lim-ited to communication from one person to another, or from one spirit to another. It can be transmitted from any energy source (a city, for example, or a country, or any body of consciousness) to any other energy source or sources (a person or any number of people, whether they know each other or not).

I suppose that in fairness I should add that any number of

experts and skeptics insist that communication through telepathy has never been proven. I'm not quite sure what they need as proof, and many of you with children who blurt out accurate information they have no way of knowing already have all the proof you need. There's a wonderful, well-documented story I love telling about a truly amazing demonstration of involuntary telepathy—i.e., the receiver had no idea at all that knowledge he'd been given had come to him telepathically. It doesn't involve children, but it will help you understand what telepathy looks like and how unlimited it is in its power. I assume that skeptics explain this story away as coincidence. As you read it, just for fun, try to imagine the astronomical odds against this particular coincidence . . . and the odds against some of the coincidences that some of you have experienced with your children, when they come up with a statement of fact they couldn't possibly have known.

There was a man named Victor Samson who was a news editor for the *Boston Globe*. One night, stressed out from a particularly high-pressured day, he did a little too much unwinding after work at a bar near work. When he staggered out a few hours later, his only thought was to get to the closest bed as quickly as possible, and so, rather than heading home, he decided to go back to the *Globe,* where he promptly passed out on his office sofa.

That night Mr. Samson had a horrifying dream about a devastating volcanic eruption on an island mountain. In his dream the island was called "Pele," and thousands of helpless residents of the villages that surrounded the mountain were killed in the fiery rivers of molten lava. The dream was so graphic, and so upsetting to Mr. Samson, that the instant he woke from it he grabbed the nearest piece of paper, which happened to be a reporter's work sheet, and wrote down every detail he could remember. Then, still disturbed by his dream and still a little hung over, he decided to go home for a few more hours of sleep before he was due back at the office again.

Early the next morning, the *Globe*'s publisher happened by Mr. Samson's office, noticed the work sheet on his desk, read the heartbreaking story of those thousands of people trapped on a tiny island, decimated by a violent volcanic eruption. Unaware that the story was nothing more than Mr. Samson's dream, the publisher urgently printed it and sent it out on wire services throughout the country.

Only later that day when Mr. Samson returned to work did the publisher discover that the prestigious, highly respected *Boston Globe* had reported to all of America what amounted to nothing more than an alcohol-induced nightmare.

Weeks later a fleet of ships arrived in Boston harbor with the tragic news that on the Indonesian island of Krakatau, an island the natives called Pele, a volcanic explosion had killed almost 40,000 people, within the same hours in which Mr. Samson had his dream.

In today's world there would be a thousand explanations for that information reaching Mr. Samson so immediately, even while he slept: his office TV was on, his office radio was on, he glanced at his computer in his sleep without remembering.

But Mr. Samson's tragically accurate dream happened in August of 1883. No TVs, no radios, no computers, no electronic way at all for Mr. Samson to receive the news from halfway around the world.

Which leaves nothing but the alternative explanation: He was given the news through the theoretically unproven phenomenon of telepathy.

Children also receive an enormous amount of information from the Hall of Justice by way of **infused knowledge**. Infused knowledge, like telepathy, is accurate information about the past, present, or future that's instantaneously transferred from one mind to an-

221

other without the five physical senses being involved. But unlike telepathy, the information doesn't seem to come from any specific sender. It's simply not there one second and there the next.

Abby wrote, "My daughter Darla has been psychically gifted since she was a toddler. She had just turned four when she and my husband and I were on our way to a friend's birthday party and she said, 'Daddy, I'm sorry about your brother.' He asked her what she meant and she answered, and these were her exact words, 'He went to heaven when he was only ten.' My husband was so shocked that he actually pulled the car over and stopped. Even I didn't know until then that when my husband was eight years old, his ten-year-old brother died of leukemia. It was such a tragedy that no one in his family ever spoke of it, and I'm sorry to say we weren't church-goers at the time and I'm sure she never heard about heaven in our home. He was careful to make sure she knew she wasn't in trouble when he asked her who told her about his brother. She sounded genuinely confused when she said, 'Nobody did. God just wanted me to say it.' "

"My daughter Kaylie's Grandpa Jim died a couple of years before she was born," wrote John. "We kept a display of small framed family photos on the shelves of our entertainment center, and one day Kaylie picked up a photo of him on a fishing trip and said, 'Grandpa Jim's favorite game was chess, but I don't know how to play.' I just stood there and stared at her. My father, 'Grandpa Jim,' was a statewide chess champion. I asked if someone in the family told her that, or—I do believe that our departed loved ones are around us—if maybe Grandpa Jim told her. She shook her head. I said, 'Then how did you know that, Kaylie?' She told me, 'Everybody knows that, Daddy,' like it was the dumbest question she ever heard."

You'll often find that children who receive information telepathically will be specific about who told them—most typically a departed loved one or their imaginary playmate (usually their Spirit Guide)—while they'll be unable to pinpoint the exact source of infused knowledge. But the truth is, it's not always easy—or necessary—to tell whether a child's accurate information came to them through telepathy or infused knowledge, or even through their own astral travel to the infinite resources of the Hall of Records on the Other Side. All that really does matter in the end is that if the information—past, present, or future—turns out to be factual, you don't have to spend another moment wondering where it came from or how they knew. You can eliminate lucky guesses and coincidences, and you can stop worrying that there's something wrong or abnormal or weird about your child. At the heart of it all are God's gifts to His children, expressing themselves by His perfect, logical design, requiring no more comment from you than your prayers of gratitude.

The Gift of Psychometry

"My brother Charles is a highly respected surgeon who could never be bothered with any kind of spiritual or psychic 'nonsense,'" wrote Marlene. "If something couldn't be scientifically studied, researched, tested, and proved, it wasn't worth believing in or talking about. Because of that I never discussed with him my daughter Lola's constant experiences with spirits from the time she was born. He was just crazy about her as his only niece, and she was just as crazy about him. One day when she was about four years old she walked into the kitchen to find Charles and me talking quietly, and she became very upset because he was crying. His wife, Joan, Lola's aunt, had just been diagnosed with cancer, and he came to me to 'vent' so that Joan wouldn't see how frightened he was. On hearing

223

this news Lola asked Charles if he had something that belonged to Joan that she could hold. We assumed it was just a gesture of fear or sentimentality or love of her aunt—we didn't really know why she wanted it. But Charles had Joan's keychain with him, with her house and car keys on it, so he handed it to Lola. She held it and closed her eyes, and after a few seconds she suddenly informed her that Joan would go through several surgeries and be very sick for a while, but in the end she would survive the cancer and it would go away. Then she gave the keychain back to Charles and left the room. We were both in shock and didn't know what to make of that. But it turned out that Joan went through several surgeries and was very sick for a while, all of which she survived, and then two years later she was declared 'completely clean'—the cancer was gone. Lola had never done anything like that before, but of course the rest of the family heard about it, and there were at least another four or five times over the years when she would hold an object belonging to a family member, at their request, and tell them something about their health, or about a new job that was coming, or about where they could find something they'd misplaced. We all treated it like it was kind of a family game, but game or not, she was right every single time, and nobody's a bigger believer in her 'special skill' these days than her uncle, my surgeon brother Charles."

Vicki shared a similar story about her almost-three-year-old son, Todd. "My closest childhood friend, Becky, made some serious mistakes after we both became adults, and she spent a year in prison for embezzling thousands of dollars from her employer. I'm a widow, raising my young son Todd on my own, and I can guarantee that Becky was always spoken of with nothing but love in my home. I wanted to help her get back on her feet after her prison term, believing that good people do stupid things sometimes and she deserved a second chance, so when she asked if she could spend a week at my house until her new apartment was ready, I welcomed her into my home. While she was settling in a few minutes after she got there, she happened to drop her wallet. Todd picked it up, and before he handed it back to her I saw a frown cross his little face. He and I quickly left to run some errands. Becky stayed at the house to take a nap. When Todd and I were alone in the car I was still thinking about that frown I'd seen, and I asked him if everything was okay. He answered, 'She bad.' I was surprised, because I thought they hit it off so well, so then I asked him what made him say such a thing. His answer to that was, 'Her purse.' (He didn't know the difference yet between a wallet and a purse.) I didn't understand, and I should have asked him more questions about it, but I didn't; I just gave him a talk about how much he'd like her when he got to know her and how it wasn't right to judge people so quickly. I found out the hard way that he obviously got some sort of bad feeling when he had her wallet in his hand, because we got home two hours later to find Becky gone, along with my jewelry and most of my clothes."

These two stories illustrate two different results of exactly the same psychic gift. It's called psychometry, and it's the ability to sense and interpret the living energy that's been absorbed by inanimate objects. Perceptions of that energy can come in the form of visions, smells, sounds, emotions, and even specific empathetic physical sensations like pain, heat, and cold.

In Chapter Three you read about imprints, the collective emotional energy, positive or negative, that's accumulated at specific places on earth where great miracles or tragedies have occurred. The energy is so powerful that it forms a vortex, which continues feeding on itself and permeates everything around it, both living and nonliving. On a small, mundane scale, the inanimate objects around us are capable of becoming miniature imprints as well, absorbing the energy of those who've had extended contact with them and then transmitting the same energy to those who are sensitive to it. And those who are sensitive to that energy and can accurately translate it are said to have the gift of psychometry.

Psychics who specialize in psychometry when working with law enforcement, for example, can hold an article of a missing child's clothing and, by reading the child's energy contained in that clothing, receive images or smells or sounds from where the child is, sense whether the child is feeling frightened or is with someone who makes them feel secure, and/or perceive any injuries the child might have.

The children in the two letters you read earlier were able to hold objects owned by specific people and come up with two different kinds of readings about the energy emanating from the object. The first child was sensitive to, and accurate about, a serious health issue and the course it would take. The second child simply picked up negative energy, knew it, and communicated it very effectively despite his limited vocabulary.

And here's a little aside to show you how much even specific psychic skills like psychometry vary in their interpretations from one person to the next. Many years ago I taught a course in psychic development at De Anza College near San Francisco. When we focused on psychometry, as part of the overall lesson that different people receive messages in different ways, I had each student bring me an object to hold. My sole request was that they be armed with facts about the owners of the objects—one of my most basic beliefs about the psychic world is that any information a psychic receives is worthless unless it's validated sooner or later. Without validation, it's just guesswork, and let's face it, anyone can say anything they want.

Psychics have to be held to a high percentage of accuracy or there's no value to what we have to offer.

In my experiences with psychometry during those courses at De Anza College, I was able to very accurately read the past and present of the object's owner when I held the object in my hand. But to read anything about their future, I had to set the object aside and rely on my other skills. So I'm always impressed when I read about someone, especially a child, who's able to use psychometry to receive valid future information.

At any rate, if you have a child who's skilled at psychometry, take their impressions into account, obviously, but don't make decisions based solely on the messages they give you. That's not because the messages can't necessarily be trusted; it's because it's much too much responsibility to place on a child's shoulders. Ageless spirits as they are, children are still feeling their way around this particular earthly lifetime. So as psychically and spiritually gifted as a child might be, never forget to let them be children, and never forget that they need adult guidance and nurturing as much as every other child. And when it comes to specific gifts, like psychometry, which can be great sources of fascination to adults when they start manifesting themselves, be very careful not to imply that you'll be disappointed in them if they don't get a hit on every object they hold or on every psychic question they're asked.

My friend and cowriter Lindsay and I still chuckle about a day years ago when she and Angelia were spending the day at my office. The mail arrived, and Angelia was thrilled that one of the letters was addressed to "Sylvia Browne and Angelia Dufresne." (Angelia had appeared on *The Montel Williams Show* with me a couple of times, and we had mentioned on the air that she was already showing some remarkable psychic abilities.) The letter was from a distraught woman whose ten-year-old son had been missing for several months, and she was asking if Angelia and I could help find him.

Lindsay read the letter aloud to Angelia and then said, "What do you think, Eya, do you have any ideas about where this little boy might be?"

To which Angelia replied, in her patented "wow, are you an idiot" tone, "I'm *six,* Lindsay."

A good reminder to all of us: No matter how extraordinary the talents, in this or any other area, never forget the words *age appropriate.*

And if you find yourself worrying that your psychometrically gifted child is odd and/or abnormal, please take this into account before you overreact: To some degree or other, you, and the rest of us, have psychometric skills as well, and you use them regularly. If you've ever picked up an attractive item while shopping that's exactly what you'd been looking for, let's say, and found that when you held it there was something about it that made you put it back and keep looking, that's psychometry. If you've ever gone apartment hunting or house hunting, sincerely needing to move, and found a place that seemed perfect in every way, but for some reason you passed it up because it didn't feel right, that's psychometry. If there's a family heirloom in your house that you know you're supposed to cherish, but it makes you uneasy even though you don't know why and you'd secretly love to sell it on eBay, that's psychometry. And by the way, I won't let something stay in my house for five minutes if I find myself having a negative psychometric response to it, no matter how expensive it is or how much someone else in my family once adored it or how often I'm told that it's going to be incredibly valuable someday if I'll just hang on to it. The more you pay attention to your own psychometric skills, the more value you'll find in them, even if it's only to make sure there's nothing around you that even slightly interferes with your emotional, psychic, and spiritual comfort.

As you watch your child develop their own psychometric skills, particularly if the skills are advanced enough for them to give you accurate information about the owners of the objects they're reading, it's essential that you clarify for them (and for yourself, in case it's not obvious) that it's the absorbed energy in the objects that's creating their response to them. When their response is a negative one, it doesn't mean for one moment that the objects themselves are haunted or possessed or evil. Spirits and ghosts can manipulate inanimate objects, and they can contribute to the energy held inside them, but they can't occupy them. *Inanimate* means "not alive," and "not alive" means they're uninhabitable for anything living, from earth or from the spirit world. Psychometrically gifted children are detecting and communicating nothing more and nothing less than the energy of an object's owner. Beyond that, the object itself is irrelevant, only a tool that children with this particular gift find psychically useful to read.

Clairsentience

We discussed clairvoyance, clairaudience, and clairsentience in the first chapter, but they're worth another mention here, particularly clairsentience and one of the forms it commonly takes in children.

Clairvoyance, you probably recall, is the ability to see beings, objects, or information from another dimension. Clairaudience is the ability to hear those same beings, objects, or information. Clairsentience is the ability to accurately read and often personally experience the physical and emotional energy of spirits from both other dimensions and this one.

A letter from Susan represents dozens I received with very similar themes and very similar confusion. "At the age of four," she wrote, "my son Gerald began showing a weird ability to read people's palms. The first time it happened we were having dinner with my sister Anita and her new boyfriend, Brad. Gerald was sitting next to Brad, and all of a sudden in the middle of casual dinner conversation Gerald took Brad's hand, turned it so the palm was facing up, looked at it like he was studying it, and said, 'You're not supposed to hit people, you know.' You can imagine how shocked we all were, to the point where Brad just sat there for a minute and then got up and ran out of the restaurant. My sister ran out after him, and I asked Gerald what made him say such a thing. He said he 'saw it in [Brad's] hand' that he hit people when he got mad, and 'he should stop it.' I agreed that Brad should stop it if it was true, but it wasn't the kind of thing you just blurt out to people, and it wasn't nice to hurt people's feelings like that. Gerald promised to apologize to my sister and Brad.

"Well, it turned out he didn't owe any apologies. Anita called the next day to say that because of how upset he was over Gerald's announcement, Brad confessed to her that he had a history of convictions for domestic abuse. He told her the incidents were 'misunderstandings' and he only pleaded guilty to avoid trials and 'get it over with' because 'the system always railroads the man in situations like that.' My sister wasn't buying it and broke up with him that same night. She finally had to take out a restraining order on Brad, but that's another story for another time.

"The point is, Gerald has been reading palms of friends and family members ever since. He can tell when people are having health problems, or when they're stressed out or angry about something, or when they're sad, or when they're especially happy about something, or even when they're pregnant as my aunt found out she was after Gerald told her. He's seven years old now, and we're very careful not to let people take advantage of his gift, because what we want most for him is to just be a normal little boy.

"We would love to understand what's going on with him, though. Most of the time he's the most typical seven-year-old you've ever seen, but in this one area it's like he's a little alien or something. Should we let him keep going with this, or put a stop to it? All we care about is what's best for him, if we only knew what that is."

I'm sure there are a lot of palmists (palm readers) who would disagree with what I'm about to say, but I strongly believe that what this child, and genuinely gifted adult palmists, experience has nothing to do with palms and everything to do with clairsentience. I believe what they're really reading is the energy of the person with whom they're in physical contact by holding their hand to study their palm. Similar letters discussed children who could receive accurate information about family members and friends from a hug, a comforting hand on the shoulder, or simply sitting in their laps. The key lies in the physical contact and a clairsentient child's ability to interpret the energy they're exposed to during that physical contact.

There's no real way to put a stop to a child's clairsentience, and it can serve them well when it comes to discerning between those people they're comfortable with and those they instinctively avoid. The downside of clairsentience, as I mentioned in the first chapter, is when a child actually absorbs whatever pain, illness, or negativity someone in their presence is feeling to the point where they begin to experience it themselves. It's essential that any clairsentient, child or adult, keep the boundaries very clear between their own energy

231

and the energy around them, and in the last chapter of this book you'll find useful ways to help them do that.

Apportation

Apport, or apportation, isn't a psychic gift your child might be blessed with. Instead, it's a psychic phenomenon from the spirit world that your child might easily attract. And if it happens, it might just as easily mystify you and make you question your own sanity.

Apportation is a fascinating event in which the spirit world dramatically manipulates a physical object here on earth. They may transport the object through space and/or seemingly impenetrable barriers so that it seems to materialize out of nowhere, or to disappear from a place you're absolutely certain it was and then reappear in some other place you're equally certain it can't possibly be. As much as it may sound like a cosmic practical joke at first glance, it's really the spirit world making a loud, clear, inarguable statement that they're around, they're powerful, and our earthly ideas of physics and logic aren't about to limit them in the least. We adults tend to scramble frantically around in search of some reasonable explanation, no matter how ridiculous. Children, on the other hand, tend to accept apportations as just another loving wave from Home.

Jean writes, "My mother, Ann, passed away a year before my daughter Ashley was born. Mom had a collection of teddy bears with a lot of different elaborate Elizabethan costumes. They were called William Shakesbears, and she loved them. We donated the collection to the children's wing of our local hospital while Ashley was an infant, so there's no chance she ever saw a William Shakesbear or knew what one was. One day when Ashley was two years old I was shopping with her at Toys "Я" Us. She was sitting in the cart, and my back was turned to her while I checked out a shelf of dolls. After a minute or two I heard her say, 'Want this Mama.' I looked to see what she was talking about and she was holding a William Shakes-bear with a beautiful plum-colored brocade coat and "Shakespeare" hat. It took me aback for a second before I started looking around to see what shelf she took it from, but there were no William Shakes-bears anywhere for as far as the eye could see. Then I noticed that there was no price tag on it, so I figured some child or someone had given it to her as they passed by, but in my heart I knew no one had passed us in the short time my back was turned. Ashley was hugging that bear as tight as she could, and I finally asked her where it came from. Clear as a bell she said, 'Nana Ann' (our family nickname for my mom), and I burst into tears right there in the middle of the aisle. I believed then and I'll always believe that my mother was with us that day and by some miracle I'll never understand she gave my daughter that unmistakable little bear. (I since found out that William Shakesbears were discontinued fifteen years before Ashley was born.)"

That miracle is a perfect example of an apportation in which an object seemed to simply appear out of thin air, when in fact Jean was exactly right—her mother personally delivered it, as a way of saying, "I'm watching over my granddaughter, and if you don't believe it, explain this."

Just as dramatic was a story from Stella, about an apportation in which an object was transported from one place to another when it seemed impossible. "My husband's parents, Earl and Janis, drove six hundred miles to attend our beautiful baby daughter Emma's baptism. They spent several days with us, and at the end of their visit I helped my mother-in-law, Janis, pack to leave, since she has very poor eyesight due to cataracts. I personally put Janis's diamond hair clip, which she wore to the baptism, into her suitcase, and I personally closed and latched her suitcase and carried it to their car. Tragically, Earl and Janis were in a terrible car accident on the way home. Earl survived but was hospitalized for several weeks, but Janis died at the scene. My husband flew there immediately. Two days later I was getting the baby and myself ready to go meet him. I opened Emma's dresser drawer to get her clothes to pack and there on top of her little T-shirts was Janis's diamond hair clip! I've gone over it in my mind a million times, and I know it had to have been in that accident with them almost six hundred miles away. I'll never get over that."

For the record, sometimes earthly explanations are the logical, correct ones, and the same is true with apportations. I'll never encourage you to believe that every time something turns up in an odd place, or gets misplaced and then found again, it's the spirit world at work. But I will encourage you to watch out for objects that suddenly, impossibly appear, or show up somewhere when you know they have to be somewhere else, especially around your children, who attract the spirit world like magnets. When and if it happens, don't dismiss it too lightly. Pay attention. Exhaust every other possible explanation. Think. Then smile to yourself, recognize the probability of an apportation, and say, "Welcome, and thank you" to that loving spirit around your child who's asking so loudly and clearly to be noticed.

Special Needs Children with Special Gifts

There are a couple of things I want to make very, very clear about children with special physical, mental, and emotional needs.

The first and most important is the horribly unfair and *completely mythical fallacy* that special needs children are paying the price, or receiving the karma, for some terrible sin they committed in a past life. Nothing could be further from the truth. In fact, the exact opposite is true.

When I say we all write detailed charts on the Other Side for the lives we're coming here to experience, I mean all of us. Yes, I mean that special needs children designed a life for themselves this time around in which they'd face challenges the rest of us can only imagine. I truly want you to *think,* and think hard, about how incredibly advanced these spirits have to be to choose such extraordinary challenges for themselves. By comparison, the rest of us are still in kindergarten when it comes to our eternal spiritual wisdom. These children, these brilliantly advanced courageous spirits, deserve all the love, support, and profound respect we can give them, and our gratitude for the extraordinary examples they set for all of us just by being here.

The second point is that more often than not, special needs children are every bit as special when it comes to their psychic gifts. Like all other children, they're newly arrived from and still partly residents of the spirit world of the Other Side. As we've just established, they're also spiritually advanced and, as a result, more finely tuned to the higher frequency of the spirit world. And because, typically, one or more of special needs children's physical and mental

235

senses are impaired or disabled, others of their senses (including psychic ones) are heightened, not to mention that there will be less earthly interference for the spirit world's signals to be filtered through.

From Karen: "My five-year-old daughter, Kimmy, is autistic. A few months ago my father, Kimmy's "Pawpaw," died of heart failure. I was home with Kimmy and several family members, while my husband, mother, and other family members kept vigil at the hospital. We were all doing our best to be as normal and upbeat as possible and act as if nothing upsetting was going on, since we didn't want to tell Kimmy about her grandfather until the inevitable had happened. But suddenly Kimmy stood up and went to every person in the room, pulled us to our feet, and insisted we form a circle holding hands. She began breathing very heavily, put her hand on her chest and said it hurt. That only lasted for a couple of moments. Then she breathed normally again and took her hand off her chest and said, 'Don't cry for Pawpaw.' It was less than ten minutes later that my husband called to say my father had slipped away."

Mary wrote, "My son Stephan has Asperger's Syndrome, which is an autism-spectrum disorder. When he was eight years old he passed by me one day and said, "I want you to have another baby, Mom." I didn't have the heart to tell him that his father and I had gone to the urologist a week earlier to discuss the possibility of a vasectomy, so I just explained that we'd need a bigger bank account and a bigger house to handle another child and I was sorry I couldn't honor his request. He was insistent about this new baby, and he wasn't happy with me for being just as insistent that it wasn't going to happen. He let it go for the time being, but a couple of days later he told me again that he wanted me to have a baby, and it would be a boy. I repeated that it wasn't going to happen and that this subject

236

was no longer up for discussion, period. He replied, 'Well, it's too late!' and went to his room. What he said alarmed me, and I could feel the hair on the back of my neck standing on end when I followed him to his room and asked what he meant by that. He said he didn't know. His Asperger's makes it difficult to elaborate on anything, so I left it alone. But two weeks later I found out I was pregnant, and eight months later I gave birth to a healthy baby boy."

"My autistic daughter, Mimi, is four years old," wrote Kara. "I've read a few of Sylvia's books, and one day out of curiosity from those books I asked Mimi where she goes when she dreams. She said, 'I go home, of course.' She also talks about several interesting things she's done, but I can attest to the fact that she's never done them in this life. Then a couple of days ago she began addressing her sister Brianne by the name 'Vivian.' I asked her why she was suddenly calling her sister 'Vivian' instead of Brianne and she said, 'Because that was her name a long time ago.'"

"My son Will has cerebral palsy. He's the joy of my life and I can honestly say one of the most interesting people I've ever known, child or adult. He's talked and laughed and played since he was an infant with all sorts of friends I can't see. Other family members are surprised that things like that don't upset me, but how can I be upset at anything that makes him so happy? He also says fascinating things on a regular basis, and I was so glad I had a witness for the most recent one. It was the day before Will's fourth birthday, and he and my sister and I were out picking up decorations for his party. Out of nowhere he started picking up various decorations and saying, 'Gampa Oscar likes this one, and this one, and this one.' His Gampa Oscar, my father, died two years before Will was born, but we always made sure Will knew who his Gampa Oscar was, so my sister and I assumed Will was just being playful and silly and excited about his birthday. On the way home he said, 'Gampa Oscar was ninety-four when he went to heaven.' My sister and I gave each other a shocked look, because my father was indeed ninety-four when he died, and then I asked, 'How did you know that, Will?' His answer was, 'He just told me.' "

From Lilah: "My son Anthony was born blind and with brain damage. The doctors only expected him to live for a few weeks, but he's almost seven years old now. From the time he was an infant he would sit and laugh and talk as though someone was in his room with him during the night. As he got older, when he'd hear us talking about someone we knew who was ill, he would immediately announce the outcome of the illness, saying either, 'They're going to get better,' or, 'They're going to heaven.' And he was right every single time."

Gretchen wrote, "I have a precious four-year-old son named Ethan who has autism. He doesn't really talk or interact with people, but he seems to laugh a lot when he's alone in his room at night, as if he's playing with someone and they're tickling him. And he seems to hear and react to a lot of things that I can't hear at all. The most apparent one is the phone. Ethan always, and I mean *always*, starts running to answer the phone, no matter what room of the house we're in, but only when he's about halfway to the phone does it actually start ringing!"

From Priscilla: "I'm writing about my son Jonathan, who has cerebral palsy and mild retardation. From the time he was two years old he could tell my husband and me who called while we were on family outings and whose voices we would find on our answering machine when we got home, and he was never wrong, not once. He's always told us there are spirits around him, and we've seen him talking and laughing and playing with them many, many times when he didn't know we were watching. One evening when he was four years old Jonathan was in the family room watching TV when he suddenly started yelling, 'Mom! Mom!' I ran in to see what was wrong. Jonathan looked frightened as he told me that a man with 'hair on his face, and a white long shirt, and glowing eyes' had come in through the back door 'and he didn't even have to open it.' I asked where the man went, and Jonathan pointed to the backyard, so I ran outside and frankly wasn't surprised not to find anyone out there. Before I went back in I happened to glance over at the garage and noticed that the outdoor lights had formed the shadow of a cross on the wall. I admit, I didn't pay much attention to that either. We were never a religious, church-going family, and we had rarely mentioned God to Jonathan, let alone anything else. Jonathan was still agitated when I went back in the house, so to calm him down I got out some magazines and, as an afterthought, an old family Bible and started leafing through the pictures, asking Jonathan to show me if anyone looked like the man he saw. We went through all the magazines and he didn't say a thing. We were almost through the pictures in the Bible when he got very excited and said, 'Mom, *that's him!*' It was a picture of Jesus Christ. Just the idea that my sweet, disabled little boy might have had a visitation from Christ made me cry, and from that night on he's begged us to take him to church, which we do whenever we possibly can. I always thought I was here to teach Jonathan. Now I'm sure that he's here to teach me."

I have nothing to add to that except to say, "Please, God, help all of us with children in our lives take every opportunity to let them teach us."

CHAPTER NINE

When a Child Goes Home

There is nothing more devastating than the death of a child. No words in any earthly language are adequate to describe the pain of the void it creates in our hearts, and in a world that's immeasurably diminished by even the smallest loss of innocence and hope. It offends our sense of order and fairness—the old are *never* supposed to bury the young. In our darkest moments it can corrupt our faith in a loving, compassionate God, when it seems that there's nothing but cruelty and selfishness in taking a child from our arms in the name of God's will.

But because He is a loving, compassionate God, no matter how much faith you might lose in Him, He will never lose faith in you. And no child has ever gone Home because of some random unilateral whim of His that leaves us decimated. I promise you from the core of my soul that when a child returns to the Other Side, to resume their busy lives of perfect, blissful peace, it's because, impossible as it seems in someone so young, they've completed their chart, that part of their eternal journey that they came here to accomplish.

Throughout this book we've talked about the detailed life charts we write before we come here, to guarantee that we achieve the goals that brought us here in the first place. It's a natural assumption that those goals are always obvious and always for ourselves. But just as often, they're for some greater good, some ultimate difference only we could have made by being here, however briefly. Sometimes, for the advancement of our spirits, we chart a life in which we really are here to teach more than to learn, knowing that only on earth is death perceived as the ultimate tragedy. In the context of the eternity God's promised us, it's simply a transition, nothing more and nothing less than one more joyful, sacred Homecoming. And still in close proximity to the spirit world from which they just arrived, no one remembers that more clearly, doubts it less, and understands it more deeply than a child. The rest of us, left behind to grieve, know it too; we've just been away from Home so long that we've temporarily forgotten.

I once had the honor of knowing a child named Abby. Abby's mother developed a severe illness during pregnancy, and Abby was born blind, deaf, and mute. Abby's parents worked long, hard hours for the little money they had, and her eleven older siblings essentially grew up on their own, wild, unsupervised, and undisciplined, self-absorbed and chronically in every kind of trouble they could find.

I met this lost, seemingly hopeless family before Abby was born, when it looked as if her mother might not survive giving birth to her. I saw the emptiness in their eyes; I saw their lack of purpose; I saw how and why they'd lost their belief that the next day would be any different or better than the day before; and I saw that it had been so long since they'd seen any good reason to love themselves that they'd lost sight of how much they loved each other.

Abby's mother miraculously survived giving birth to this tiny, black-haired, precious baby, and one by one the children came into the hospital room, desperately relieved to see her and hold their new sister. One by one they were told that Abby was blind, deaf, and mute. And one by one their hearts opened up to the helpless innocence they held in their arms, who had nothing to offer them but her complete trust and her unconditional love. She reignited their compassion, she gave each of them a purpose and a sense of commitment, and she united them into a family again. Without ever saying or hearing a single word, or seeing a single one of their faces, she simply loved them and, because of that, she made each of them feel worth being loved.

Abby died of pneumonia at the age of eight. And in her short time on this earth, there's not a doubt in my mind that she fulfilled every word of the chart she wrote: She transformed thirteen desolate people into the most caring, giving, hardworking, spiritual family I've ever known. How can any of us doubt that it was worth the trip for her, and that she went Home in the sacred, joyful peace of a spirit who only stopped by this time around to leave this world a little more loving and compassionate than she found it?

So never believe that there's any such thing as a child who was taken too soon, or whose time here was too brief to be of value. Taken too soon for us, absolutely. But for them? They're on the Other Side again, safe, whole, and happy, knowing they made a difference somewhere, somehow, a difference that will become more and more apparent to us as our grief for them begins to subside.

Exit Points

You might also find some comfort in knowing that, just like all of us, children participate in the decision about when it's time for them to go Home.

When we write our charts on the Other Side for an upcoming lifetime, we design them based on the goals we've set for ourselves. We may not be sure how long it will take us to accomplish those goals. But we're very sure that however long or short a time it takes, we're not embarking on this rough visit to earth without guaranteeing that we can head Home again—essentially, that we haven't inadvertently bought ourselves a one-way ticket instead of a round trip. And so, to cover ourselves no matter what the circumstance, we write five different exit points into our charts, five separate opportunities to exit this life when we're satisfied that our reasons for coming here have been realized.

Writing five exit points into our charts doesn't mean we're obligated to wait around for the fifth one to play itself out. We might decide when our first exit point comes along, or our second, or fourth, that we've done all we hoped for on this trip. And we don't necessarily space them out evenly when we create them. We might write in two exit points for the same year, for example, and then have twenty or thirty years to wait until our next one comes along.

The most obvious exit points include critical illnesses and surgeries, or potentially fatal accidents that can range from a fall from our crib to a car wreck to a skydiving mishap to combat on the front lines in Iraq—any event that could result in our death. Those situations in which we should have died but didn't are simply exit points we chose not to take.

Other exit points are so subtle that we might not even recognize them: deciding for no reason to drive a different route than usual to work; trivial delays that keep us from leaving the house on time; a last-minute change in travel plans; canceling a commitment because we suddenly just don't feel like it. Countless incidents that seem unimportant at the time can easily be our spirit's memory of an exit point we wrote into our chart but decided not to take advantage of after all.

Five choices, ours to make, of when and how to leave this life. And when a child goes Home, I promise you, they've simply opted for the first of those five choices or exit points. Which guarantees that whatever it is they came here to do, they did it and did it well enough to be at total peace when they leave.

A Child's Trip to the Other Side

I've done thousands upon thousands of past-life regressions with clients from every culture and every religion on earth. I can't begin to guess the number of clients who, during those regressions, remembered a few past lives that ended when they were children. And every one of them, no matter what their specific beliefs, describes exactly the same experience when their spirit left their body: They cross a footbridge into an impossibly beautiful meadow, where everyone they've ever loved in all their past lives on earth and on the Other Side, and every animal they've ever loved as well, are waiting to joyfully welcome them Home. They're exhilarated to be free of their earthly bodies again, to feel whole and strong and perfect, to be reunited with their natural state of bliss, to live among the Messiahs and the Angels, and to breathe in the purest, sweetest-smelling air that is virtually alive itself, infused as it is with the immediate, holy presence of God's peaceful grace.

They resume their busy, happy lives, watching over us, visiting us whether we're aware of them or not, leaving us countless signs we can easily miss in the dark, numb pain of grief. Like all their beloved brothers and sisters in the spirit world, they might leave coins in the most unlikely places. They might turn lights, appliances, televisions, and computers on and off. They might stop clocks, make phones and doorbells ring, play music boxes, turn on toys with supposedly dead batteries, manipulate photographs around the house, move car keys and other small essential items from a place we *know* we put them to a place that makes no sense at all, they might take a seat on the sofa or the edge of the bed that we don't even notice until we look to see a slight indentation that wasn't there before. They can send birds, butterflies, and other animals to visit on their behalf. They can make you swear you felt a subtle breath on the back of your neck, or a tiny breeze in your hair when the air around you is perfectly still.

They can visit or send signs at any time, but pay special attention during rainstorms or in the early morning hours before dawn. Electricity and water, in the form of lightning, rain, humidity, or dew, are conductors of energy. And spirits are energy, after all. These conductors aren't essential to visits and signs from your child, but they can make the trip between dimensions easier and increase the frequency with which they occur.

The question I'm asked most often about any deceased loved one who's gone Home is "Are they happy?" Please listen to me, especially those of you whose children have returned to the Other Side, when I say, "YES!" I don't need to hear your particular case, or be in direct contact with you, or see a photograph of your child to be able to tell you that. It's not a psychic answer; it's a spiritual one. Whether you call it Home, or the Other Side, or heaven, your child is alive and well in a place where there is no illness, no sorrow, no worries, no regrets, no fear, no loneliness. Would it be heaven if any of those things were even possible? I promise, any doubts you might have about that are your own projections, from the limited perspective of earthly sadness and grief. They're not real when it comes to your child, who left all negativity behind at the moment they left their body and this hard, flawed world.

And then there's the question "Does my child miss me?" I really want you to understand and celebrate that the answer is "No." That answer has nothing to do with you and everything to do with the fact that each and every one of us is living an eternal life. There are few things harder for us to grasp on earth than eternity, the reality that we always have been and always will be, that there is no such thing as time, or an inevitable beginning, middle, and end; there is only a perpetual NOW. But everywhere else but here, we understand it perfectly. It's our natural backdrop. In computer terms, it's our default. And it's in the context of eternity that your child on the Other Side is thriving. They're not wondering if they'll see you again; they *know* they will, and while to you it will seem like an agonizing stretch of time until you're together again at Home, greeting each other in that impossibly beautiful meadow, to them it will be less than the blink of an eye. Conceptually, think of it as maybe less than a second in the course of a decade, or a century, less time than you can even notice between now and when that thrilling reunion will take place. If you knew that in less than a second you'd be reuniting with someone you love, would missing them be an issue? Of course not. It's exactly the same with your child. Even if your death won't be happening for another fifty or eighty or a hundred years, your child perceives it as less than a second away, and they're probably busy planning your Homecoming party right now.

Grief

I wish I had some wonderful exercises and words of wisdom to help you through your grief at the loss of a child, or at least to lessen its duration. But sadly, surviving grief is one of the reasons we chose to experience yet another life on earth. There is no grief on the Other Side, so this is the only place we can confront it, ache from it, grow from it, and add the strength we gained from it to our eternal body of wisdom. The bottom line is, if you can think of our time on earth as school, then grief is the most difficult course we'll ever sign up for. Once you've survived grief, there's literally nothing you can't get through.

There are those who find it hard to believe that I grieve as much as anyone else. After all, I don't just have to take someone's psychic and spiritual word for it that our spirits survive death and come back from the Other Side to be with us. I can see and hear that world, and I've made countless astral trips to the Other Side and helped countless clients travel there as well.

That's all true. I don't just believe our lives are eternal; I *know* it. But that doesn't ease my grief in the least, because when I grieve, I'm not grieving for the loved ones I've lost. They're doing great, and I thank God for that. I'm grieving for *me*. I'm grieving because I miss my daddy and my Grandma Ada and my dear friends and my beloved animals, and I'm selfish enough to want them here with me. Being able to see them and hear them and find signs from them is comforting. But all of that pales in comparison to having them walk into this room I'm in right now, in the same dimension I'm in right now, and hug me and make me laugh and fill my heart with a proud, simple "That's my girl."

The point is, if you're lost in the grief of losing a child, please try to remember how innocently selfish grief is and should be. Don't add to your pain by worrying for one moment about your child's well-being. If you want details about what and how they're doing, my book *Life on the Other Side* can tell you all you need to know. But if your only concern is that they're happy, busy, at peace, visiting you whether you feel them or not, and excited to welcome you Home when the exit point of your choice comes along, I guarantee God's already taken care of that and you don't need to give it another thought. Limit your despair to how much you miss them. That's quite enough for you to handle.

There's an old wives' tale that our grieving can keep a loved one's spirit from leaving this world and transcending to its rightful place on the Other Side, and that explains why the bereaved might not feel that spirit's presence around them. Not a word of that is true. None of us is powerful enough to prevent any spirit from going Home, especially the spirit of a child—believe me, children and animals get there far faster than any of us.

Many old wives' tales, though, are the result of a tiny shred of fact, expanded to a completely mistaken conclusion, and I have a feeling this one may not be an exception. For one thing, we have no control over how soon and how often a loved one will come to visit. I saw my Grandma Ada almost immediately after she passed away, but it took Daddy eight months to show up. I was so frustrated by then, and missed him so much, that I greeted him with a thoroughly impatient "What the hell took you so long?!" To which he replied, "What do you mean? I just left!" We're the ones who are obsessed with time, don't forget. It doesn't even exist where they are, and again, I can't emphasize this enough, from the moment they arrive back Home, they're busy. So please don't get discouraged if your child doesn't appear right away, or send signs that they're around. They will, and all you have to do is be patient, keep an open mind, and pay attention.

And then there's the undeniable, unfortunate fact that grief can throw us into such an empty state of numbness that we're often emotionally and spiritually cut off from our ability to sense even the most obvious signs and visits. It's as if our Light goes out for a while, so that we're just stumbling around in the dark trying to make it from one day to the next. But as we heal and recover, the Light comes on again, we can see more clearly, and begin noticing the magic around us. That will happen too. You may have trouble believing it right now, but that's okay. I believe it enough for both of us.

In the meantime, here are a few pieces of practical advice that I hope will help you find your way to your Light again:

✳ Ask for any and all help you need, from those who love you, from qualified doctors and psychologists and members of the clergy, and from support groups with people who have walked this same dark path you're walking now and are trained to guide you through it. Accept my standing invitation to call (408) 379-7070, extension 107, twenty-four hours a day to have your name added to my prayer chain, for added support from thousands and thousands of people all over the world who've performed miracles by raising their united voices to Father and Mother God. Until you can feel your spirits and Angels and God Himself around you again, let your legions on earth hold you while you heal. And some-day, you have my word, someday you'll be strong enough to do the same for someone else.

✳ Tempting as it may be, don't anesthetize your grief with drugs and alcohol, with the possible exception of prescribed medication from a fully qualified physician or psychophar-macologist. Drugs and alcohol won't take your pain away; they'll only postpone it, and postponing grief gives it the power to rise up at its own convenience and take you down. And any legitimate doctor will confirm that when any emo-tion as strong as grief goes unexpressed and unreleased, it's guaranteed to take on some form of its own in your body and compromise your physical health. The only sane way through grief is to feel it, endure it, and get it over with.

✳ Promise yourself that every day you'll push yourself to make the most effort you can possibly manage. Even if that boils down to nothing more than getting out of bed and getting dressed, it's better than nothing at all, and you know as well as I do that if you wait until you feel like it, whatever "it" is, you're likely to be waiting a very long time. As pointless as going through the motions might seem, it will send your body the message that you're still alive and functioning, and sooner or later, your mind will follow and believe it too.

✳ Be more vigilant than ever before about avoiding any and all negativity around you and embracing everyone and every-thing that's positive, supportive, and spiritually nourishing.

Think of grief as an open emotional wound, negativity as salt on that wound, and loving support and spiritual comfort as the balm that will protect the wound and speed its healing.

✳ And finally, if you feel there was something left unsaid between you and the child who's gone Home, say it now. I promise you from the depth of my soul that they'll hear you, and that they'll be able to repeat every word right back to you the day they're back in your arms again on the Other Side.

When my beloved Daddy went Home, I knew I couldn't get through the numbing grief without a lot of extra help from God. I wrote a prayer and forced myself to reach out to Him with it every morning, even when I was too despondent to do anything but recite it. I know it helped. I know it brought me comfort. And I know that, as with all our prayers, God answered by wrapping His arms tightly around me and holding me until the darkness of mourning passed. I share it with you in the hope that it will help and comfort you as well, and let you feel God's arms around you while you heal.

Dear God, as I face my grief today, help me not to bury it but to consent to it so that when I emerge from it with your divine guidance and compassion, I'll be wiser, stronger, kinder, and more devoted to you than ever before. Even in my darkest hours, please help me remember what I know, that someday I will understand the purpose for the loss I'm grieving, and that I have an eternity to look forward to with this loved one I've lost when we're together again in the perfect joy of the Other Side. Amen.

CHAPTER TEN

Psychic Children:
The Instruction Manual

Don't you wish all children were born with little instruction manuals tied to their wrists? I know I would have appreciated it, and probably would have done a lot of things differently. And I won't presume to give you general advice about child rearing. I'm no more of an expert at that than anyone else who's raised children.

I can, however, offer specific advice about the psychic aspect of raising psychic children. None of it is complicated or time-consuming. Its purpose is to see to it that your children's psychic gifts are a positive, safe, comfortable, normal, empowering, and, above all, God-centered force in your lives. I'm confident that it will also deepen the communication between you and your children and create disciplines you'll come to treasure. Above all, it will help your child through the often overwhelming transition from the Other Side to here.

Tools of Protection

Tools of Protection are invisible suits of armor that surround us and help protect us from the negative thoughts and energy that are unavoidable in lives on earth. They don't banish negativity from our lives completely. After all, if we weren't determined for our spirits to grow by confronting and overcoming negativity, we would have stayed on the Other Side and spared ourselves the trouble of coming here in the first place. But Tools of Protection are an added barrier against negative energy, like a divine force field we create for ourselves, by doing nothing more than choosing a protective image that appeals to us and then clearly visualizing it taking shape around us.

I want you to make a habit of surrounding your children with any of the Tools of Protection listed below, or any you'd care to devise on your own. When your children are old enough, teach them to create their own Tools to protect themselves. It takes no longer than the few seconds you'll need to firmly picture the image, or images, around your children. Do it at night as you tuck your children into bed. Do it as they head out the door to play, or board the school bus, or get dropped off for day care. Do it as you climb into a car with them, or board a plane. Do it when unavoidable negative relatives, friends, and business associates come into your home. There is no such thing as using the Tools of Protection too often, and you won't find an easier, more positive habit to acquire and to teach.

And I particularly want those of you with clairsentient children to start enveloping them in this very effective invisible armor. No one needs to deflect other people's negative physical and emotional input more than clairsentients, who need all the protection they can get from the destructive energy around them.

If you don't believe Tools of Protection will actually work, try them for a week or two just to prove me wrong. They're free of charge, and they certainly won't do your children any harm. They also won't keep your children's lives free of negativity from this moment on. But Tools of Protection can and will give them added armor when they're confronted by inevitable earthly thoughts and energy that can undermine their self-confidence.

First and always, surround your children with the most sacred, powerful protection of all, the white light of the Holy Spirit. Then add any or all of the following images:

* **The Bubble of White Light.** This is a Tool that children love and can easily picture: I'm sure you remember Glinda, the Good Witch of the North, in *The Wizard of Oz,* who floated from place to place inside a beautiful blue transparent bubble. Send your children to sleep and/or out the door in the tradition of Glinda, with one variation: instead of a blue bubble, surround them with a glowing translucent sphere made of the sacred, transparent white light of the Holy Spirit.

* **The Circle of Mirrors.** Picture your children inside a perfect circle of mirrors, taller than they are and facing away from them. Positive energy is drawn toward mirrors, while negative energy is repelled by them. This Tool has particularly dramatic results in a room full of people, some of whom are complainers, pessimists, or just plain meanspirited. If you and your children are safely protected by the Circle of Mirrors, you'll notice that those people go out of their way to avoid you without knowing why.

✳ **The Golden Sword.** Picture the most exquisite golden sword you can imagine, thick and strong, with an intricately carved hilt encrusted with jewels, like the sword of Azna, the Mother God. In your mind, place this glistening sword against your children's bodies so that the hilt forms a cross over their eyebrows and the long impenetrable blade extends down the length of their bodies to their feet, as a statement of divine power over the darkness of destructive energy.

✳ **Gold and Silver Nets.** Picture fishermen's nets, made of hand-spun gold and silver gossamer, strong as steel but light as a veil of lace, their fibers sparkling with the white light of the Holy Spirit. Drape them over your children, to cover and protect them from head to toe in sacred white light. And for added protection, drape matching gold and silver nets over any negative beings in their proximity to contain and neutralize their influence.

✳ **The Dome of Light.** This is simply a magnificent dome, its curved walls and ceiling made of the radiant, translucent white light of the Holy Spirit, large enough to contain your children wherever they are—on the playground, at school, in bed, anywhere at all, since this clear, sparkling dome can be as small or as vast as you choose it to be. I especially love using the Dome of Light as a mobile car cover when I travel with my family, even if we're only traveling a few short blocks from home.

Again, you and your children can create your own Tools of Protection, and since children are brilliant at imagery, they'll love the game of visualizing their invisible negativity shields when they're old enough and you've taught them this simple, God-centered habit.

Affirmations

Affirmations are simply focused, positive assurances to your children that they're sacred, treasured descendants of the Father and Mother God, a legacy no one can ever compromise or disrupt. Don't forget, your children are newly arrived from a world in which self-doubt of any kind is nonexistent; no one is capable of an unkind thought, let alone an unkind word; and their direct connection to God is palpable in the air itself. It's an understatement to say that the impatience with which we speak to each other and treat each other on earth is a shock to the senses of a child from Home.

The common belief in this dimension is that children are too young to be affected by the negative words and energy around them. But the spirit mind inside every child is ageless, psychic, and aware of everything in their surroundings. They absorb and come to believe whatever they're told about themselves most often, just as we adults do, magnified by the fact that children haven't yet had the opportunity to develop adult defense mechanisms. If you've ever lived with some-one who's verbally or emotionally abusive, you know how hard it is to maintain your self-confidence if you're being told on a regular basis that you're stupid, or you're useless, or you're lazy, or you'll never amount to anything. Sooner or later you're likely to start believing it. As adults, to whom negativity isn't all that shocking anymore, we can combat it, through supportive friends, through therapy, through reason and logic, through finding ways to rebuild our belief in ourselves, and through distancing ourselves from the abuser if it becomes necessary.

Psychic children, though, to whom negativity is completely alien, and who've just arrived from a place where no one ever speaks a word they don't mean and every word is loving and supportive, have no defense, no context, and no means of filtering what they hear and feel. It's up to us to keep their self-love intact, and to reinforce their sacred dignity as God's beloved creations.

With those invaluable goals in mind, I urge you to make affirmations another habit in the lives of you and your children. Never send them off to sleep, or let them start their day, without an affirmation of their divine worth. If you start the habit of regularly offering affirmations when your children are dependent on you to speak on their behalf, they can stay in the habit as they become more and more able to speak for themselves. Keep the affirmations simple and direct. Use the handful of examples that follow or compose your own. But take a moment every single day and every single night to give your children this essential spiritual nourishment, and don't forget to notice how much of that nourishment begins to enrich your own spiritual life as well.

My beautiful child, I affirm to your soul that you are lit from within by the divine power of your Creator. You are a part of God, and God is a part of you. Nothing on this earth can diminish or defeat God's living light inside you. You are loved, you are loving, and your life will be a tribute to his greatest plan for you.

My child, God has blessed me with your presence in my life, and I am humbled with joy and gratitude. When my own flaws betray that gratitude, know with all your soul that my shortcomings are mine, not yours, and close your eyes and ears to everything around you that falls short of affirming your sacred value to me and to this world.

You are a divine child of God. You are happy. You are whole. You are perfect. Great abundance will surround you throughout this lifetime in every way that truly matters because, as God's child, you are empowered with that same great abundance.

While Your Children Sleep

As we discussed at length in Chapter Six, there is no better time to speak directly to your children's spirit minds than when they're sleeping and their conscious minds are conveniently out of the way. Don't believe for a moment that they can't hear you, and that every word you say to them while they sleep doesn't have an impact. Spirit minds never sleep. They're vigilant, they're timelessly wise and educated, and they're in a constant state of growth, at their most attentive when there's no interference from their earthly minds and bodies.

Never let your children sleep without surrounding them with the white light of the Holy Spirit.

Never let them sleep without one of the Tools of Protection and always, always an affirmation.

Never let them sleep without remembering that their spirits will very probably be astrally traveling, visiting loved ones and the Home they just left behind. A prayer for those visits will help guarantee safe passage and sweet, affirming journeys, especially if your children suffer from occasional bouts of astral catalepsy.

Dearest Father and Mother God, as my child sleeps, wherever their dreams and journeys take them, may their spirit leave and return easily, without disturbing them, bringing with it assurance of your eternal, unconditional love to light every moment of their waking hours, now and forever. Amen.

Never let your children sleep without taking the opportunity to maximize the best of their cell memories and dispel the worst of them.

My beloved child, as you sleep, may you release all fear, all pain, all illness, all obstacles, whatever negativity you still cling to from past lives on earth, so that it can be resolved by God in the pure, cleansing white light of His Holy Spirit. May all the joy, love, and strength you've brought from those same lives infuse you, bless you, and empower you throughout this new lifetime in which, thank God, you've chosen me to entrust with your care.

Never let your children sleep without arming them for any nightmares and night terrors that might frighten them before they wake. You can't banish their nightmares completely—unpleasant as they are, nightmares are essential to mental health. But you can help make those nightmares more empowering.

My beautiful child, if your dreams tonight should cause you fear, may you remember to surround yourself with all your protectors, from your brave totem to your sacred legion of Angels, and face whatever scares you, knowing that nothing can defeat you because you are a treasured child of God.

And finally, never send your child to sleep with stories and lullabies, no matter how classic, in which there's even a hint of violence or scary beings of any kind who intend to cause harm. I can't tell you how many parents I've met who refuse to teach their children about the blessed, beautiful spirit world, dismissing it as either imaginary or evil, but don't hesitate to read them stories of ogres, trolls, bloodthirsty giants, and cannibalistic witches. If that makes one bit of sense to you, please rethink it, for the sake of your children's sense of peace, safety, and eternal connection to the Divine.

Inform Yourselves

I'm sure that many of you are hoping I'll give you some exercises to perform with your children when you've noticed beyond a doubt that they're blessed with psychic gifts. You want to know how to encourage, maximize, and hone those gifts, all with the very best of intentions. And it's with the very best of my intentions that I discourage psychic exercises for children and insist that you let their gifts flow naturally, at their own pace and comfort level. That's what my Grandma Ada did for me. That's what I did for my sons, Paul and Chris, and that's what Paul and Chris and I have done for my grandchildren—no exercises, no special lessons or studies, no demands or expectations beyond being happy, normal, playful children who, like all other children, happened to be psychic.

The only exercises I offer to help your psychic children, beyond the ones I've already offered in this chapter and throughout this book, are all for you:

* Keep an open mind.
* Pay attention.
* Be as supportive of their psychic talents as you'll be of every other talent with which they've been blessed.
* Arm yourselves with all the God-centered knowledge you can find about the how and why of psychic children, so that you understand their gifts and can help them understand as well.
* And finally, by all means . . .

Keep a Record

I don't care if you keep a journal or a cassette recorder on hand; whichever you'll use more reliably. But I want you to memorialize any and all of your children's psychic comments and experiences, from their imaginary playmates, to that knowledge they couldn't possibly have, to their visits from Angels and spirits who come to play with them, to their awareness of past lives, to their travels while they sleep. I promise that you and your children will come to treasure every one of these moments you preserve on their behalf.

As we've discussed throughout this book, part of the necessary design of our lives on earth is that the more time we spend here, the more we'll forget what we know of the bliss of the Other Side. We're not intended to consciously remember, or we'd do nothing but sit around impatiently waiting to go Home again where we belong.

It's healthy and inevitable that your children will forget, just as you've forgotten. But what a beautiful gift, to them and to yourself, to be able to prove to them, on paper or on tape, that once upon a time, when they were very young, they knew beyond a doubt about other lives and other dimensions and spirits and Angels and the magnificent truth of God's promise of eternity.

A Benediction

Suffer the little children to come unto me and forbid them not, for of such is the kingdom of God.

The words of Jesus, Mark 10:14

Sylvia Browne is the #1 *New York Times* bestselling author of *The Mystical Life of Jesus; Insight; Phenomenon; Prophecy; Visits from the Afterlife; The Other Side and Back; Life on the Other Side; Past Lives, Future Healing;* and *Adventures of a Psychic*. She has been working as a psychic for over fifty years and appears regularly on *The Montel Williams Show*. She has also appeared on *Larry King Live, Good Morning America,* CNN, and *Entertainment Tonight*. Visit her Web site at www.sylvia.org. She lives in California.